Norma J. Thomas

THE SMELL OF GARLIC ON SUNDAY

*a memoir,
on learning the language of feelings,
hearing what they've come to say*

Copyright © 2016
All rights reserved.

Copyright © 2016, Norma J. Thomas
All rights reserved.
This book, or parts thereof, may not be reproduced in any form, written, electronic, or live, nor adapted without written permission from holder of copyright.
Published 2016 by: Bibi's Girls Publications
Houston, TX 77090
Printed in the United States of America

Dedication

To my girls, that you may travel this journey
"through the jungle of space and time"
with your eyes open, aware that every experience
contributes to your becoming. Waste nothing, for nothing is
wasted. Go and live the life of your
extraordinary, extravagant, exquisite orchestration!

Bibi

CONTENTS

INTRODUCTION
The Smell of Garlic on Sunday
Nothing Wasted
Feelings vs Emotions, w/Disclaimer
Thank You Nuh Nuh

PROLOGUE
All in My Feelings

PART I
This Ain't No Party
No More Parties
The Retarded Class
Mama Died Last Night
Smart is All I Got
Norma Jo, Meet Racism
Don't Get Me Wrong: Checkin' In
On Being Raised, but Not Like Corn

PART II
Not Gonna Call Me a Bull Dagger
The Slow Drag Girl
Upgrade: From Invisibility to a She-Dog in Heat
Didn't I Almost Have it All?: Checkin' In
Looking for God in All the Wrong Places
Middle Finger to the Line: Checkin' In Again

CONTENTS

PART II (cont…)
And They Called it Puppy Love: I
Williams High Forensic is Groovy
Introducing Miss Lorraine Hansberry
And They Called it Puppy Love: II

PART III
Ruined
19 and Pregnant
Audacious Enough
"Remembering Kat"
Living LaVida Single Mom
I'm Coming Out
Cut High or Stay at Home: Checkin' In
Tapping the Power Within
Mother to Daughter: It's a Matter of Principle

EPILOGUE
Come 'Roun' the Mountain: Not Home Yet
Closure
Completion

ABOUT THE AUTHOR

INSTRUCTION MANUAL:
Learning the Language of Feelings

ACKNOWLEDGEMENTS

Thank you to those stalwart Black women who saw into my Spirit, taught me to seek its truth, and gave me a foundation from which to begin the journey. We called them Matrons: Deaconess Birdie Mae Tolden (posthumously), Sisters Glenda and Marie Johnson, Sis. Erma Berryman Marinovich, and Sis. Mary Tisdale Glenn (posthumously)

Thank you, also, to the Shrines of the Black Madonna of the Pan African Orthodox Christian Church for saying the very words I had been hearing in my head, having assumed I had quietly broached the threshold of insanity. In you I found Spiritual Liberation, the bridge to cross me over.

Thank you to Angela F. CeZar for not trying to change me, no matter how insane I appeared at each manifestation of myself, and for being a real partner in life.

Thank you Kam Enita for choosing me; I hope I have kept our agreement. I hope that understanding my journey will make a lot of things make sense, but most importantly, that it will inform your own. Thank you my precious girls Kamiliyah and Leelah; you give me a reason.

Thank you Pam and Joby. You were there when you were supposed to be.

Thank you Daddy for getting me here, for loving me as I slept, and when, to you, my awakenings to remembrance seemed totally "bananas".

THE SMELL OF GARLIC
ON SUNDAY

INTRODUCTION

I certainly did not know that every experience that had come into my life was depositing a treasure of feelings for the single purpose of forcing me to ask my life's question again and again in all of its many variations.

The Smell of Garlic on Sunday

To wake up on Sunday morning or walk in the door after church and Daddy's cooking Sunday dinner, the smell, sometimes coffee, most of the times, garlic, was the smell of home. We just might "eat like a family" today. Daddy might tell some jokes, or some stories. Pork roast, mustard greens, cornbread, yams, rice, something sweet to drink, no work, no school, everybody's somewhere around. It's warm. It's safe. It's home. It's what we all pine for, deep down within, that place where we feel at home, where we belong, fit in, where we are accepted for who we are. It's that place where there is no more of us that we can be because we are being all that we are; we are experiencing the highest expression of ourselves. Well, it gets pretty close to that, for most of us at least.

My own feeling of being at home was short lived, and I have come to realize that it was divinely intended. Though my father took great pains to provide a home for us, for my sisters and me, and filled that place with love and laughter, lots of laughter in the early days, I began to feel like I was having an out of body experience, or more specifically, like I was up in the rafters, looking down on my life, not really there, always craving something I could not define, requiring something I could not describe, and longing for

something I could not be provided. They say there's always that one kid in the family who sees and feels things a bit differently than all the rest. I guess I was that kid.
"Why can't we eat like a family?" A question to which laughter was the response.

"Where's Mama?" A question I well knew the answer to was but a childish way of asking, "Where's home?"
Of course, I didn't know it then.

I never felt at home anyplace. Eventually, I discovered it to be the catalyst for my life's quest and question. Where is home? Where is the fullness of myself? I searched outwardly and, ultimately, inwardly for the answers, not even aware that searching was what I was doing. I moved from one scene of my life's drama to the next, reacting, responding, trying to play the roles required, never fully understanding my motivation nor my objective. I had no idea I was moving toward anything, that there was a clear focus and direction to which I was being guided, pushed actually. I certainly did not know that every experience that had come into my life was depositing a treasure of feelings for the single purpose of forcing me to ask my life's question again and again in all of its many variations. Where is home? Where is the fullness of myself? Where is my belonging? Where is the highest expression of myself? Where is the rest of me? Where is all of me? So many deep feelings I harbored had come and kept rearing their ugly heads to keep moving me forward, until my life question was answered, or at least acknowledged and understood.

I believe, every single one of us has a life question, a theme, a focus for our existence. Every single one of us on the planet is moving toward something, going somewhere we chose before crossing the threshold into life, into embodiment. This destination is not a physical location, but a state of being. Most of us go through what we first perceive to be a bunch of crap in our lives until we come to the conclusion that it's all serving a purpose. Some, like I, determine that we are on a journey toward something, and all that crap is serving the journey. We, then, come to the awareness that the journey, is a journey of becoming, of moving toward a state of being. We, humans, physical embodiments, with our physical minds, think it's crap. We, souls being animated by the Spirit of creation, know that it's all good. And that part of us does its level best to convince us.

Some people get to their question quickly; thus, they get on to the answer, and actually live the answer. For me, it wasn't until these feelings had taken the wheel of my life, on an uphill journey, and the ride had become so crazy, so cyclical that I had to step back and take a look at it. It was in taking this time to examine my life that I perceived something divine at work, all things working together for some greater good, around a specific theme … the smell of garlic on Sunday … home … the state of being home.

Nothing Wasted

It's said all the time, "Everything happens for a reason". I've said it a number of times myself. Sometimes, it's not so easy to accept. Saying that everything happens for a reason is not intended to excuse perpetrators of attack or assault against another from their actions any more than it is intended to force the victims to deny their pain and suffering. Still, I am a firm believer that things just don't happen all willy nilly. The sunrise and the sunset, the changing of the seasons, the birth of a newborn and his growth into adulthood remind me that there is a wondrous order to the universe. Even if we are all making it up as we go along through collective thought, word, and deed, even if we just don't remember setting this whole system in motion, whether we were cosmic dust shape-shifting, alien life forms exploring, or one energy field inhaling and exhaling divine breath, it seems to me that we did whatever we did for a reason.

I've heard it said a few times this week that "no experience is wasted". Where we go, what we see, the people we encounter, the challenges we face, the efforts we take to overcome, or not, they all serve a purpose. From being born African American, a descendant of slaves, born female as the Age of Innocence in America was coming to an end, its mask to be torn away by the impending social upheaval of the Civil Rights Movement, during the boom of the birth rate in this country, born to and through a mother who would not live to provide that grounding and completion only a mother can give, to becoming a very dark child, internally and externally, a budding artist when artistry was praised from a distance and just weird up close, the experiences of my life were specifically magnetized to keep my mind, body, and soul moving in one divine direction. No experience was wasted.

Once at least embracing the notion that experiences are drawn into our lives for a purpose, that though they may range from the ridiculous to the sublime, none are wasted, one might be able to recognize that specific feelings resulted from these experiences. One might begin to examine the possibility that it's really the feelings engendered by our experiences that matter most, that impact our lives most significantly.

"Oh, the things we have felt in this unkind house that we have to tell the world about" (Lorraine Hansberry, To Be Young, Gifted, & Black). Oh, the feelings I have felt throughout my life experiences, persistent and prevailing, that never seemed to go away. Even after the misgivings were forgiven, the misunderstandings were understood, the feelings lingered, took up residence, and shaped how I viewed myself, my place in the world, and my relationship to it. We are often told to ignore our feelings, but upon seeking direction in my life, upon crafting and creating dreams, goals, and aspirations, only to find life a treadmill, getting me nowhere and nothing but the same results, trying to make sense of it all, I discovered certain feelings lurking in the shadows, common denominators. It was clear that "in my feelings" was where I needed to be. I discovered that those deep seated feelings had been trying to communicate with me, trying to tell me something, but they had a language of their own and I needed to learn it. I had been attempting to craft the life journey I desired, but I was already on a journey; there was a theme to it, a divine destination, and neither the experiences of that journey, nor the feelings they left behind, were to be wasted. In fact, they would bring the journey of my desire and the journey of my life's question into divine alignment.

Feelings vs Emotions

What I am talking about is beyond emotion. The internet is chock full of writings on the difference between feelings and emotions, but the best explanation I can give is that feelings are what come after the emotion. Feelings are emotional residue. While emotions, impulsive, conditioned, will pass, the feelings one is left with, the residual effect takes up residence in the psyche. Emotions are fluid, malleable, dependent upon conditions; some call e-motion, energy in motion, constantly moving and changing. They come. They go. Feelings settle in.

Funny story to illustrate:

We were in Branson, Missouri at the Silver Dollar City amusement park. My oldest granddaughter, 4 years old, was sobbing crocodile tears because she would not be able to get onto the next ride with the love of her life, her eight year old cousin, Taishyn. My heart went out to her because she had been such a trooper that day, trying any and everything the big kids tried. She was fearless! To distract her from her sorrow, I called out, "Kamiliyah! Can Bibi get a picture of her big girl?" In an instant, the crying stopped and Kamiliyah struck a pose. The great despair and heartbreak were gone, just like that. As we all turned into the next little eatery to get lemonade, her tears dried in the

Missouri heat, and the outburst of emotions passed on to emotion heaven, or where ever it is they can go so quickly. Emotions linger only when we choose to hold on to them; it is in their nature to move on; they are energy in motion. But they leave their mark behind; we call them feelings.

Kamiliyah Mahira Washington, not 10 seconds before this pose, was crying her eyes out. And there she is now, graduating to Middle School, 6th grade.

Dr. Antonio Damasio, neuroscientist and professor at University of Southern California explains it this way, and I like it.

> *Emotions play out in the theater of the body.*
> *Feelings play out in the theater of the mind.*

Like a lot of kids in school, I was bullied. I was made fun of; I was lied on and falsely accused, from Kindergarten to High School. Of course, Middle School was the worst, and High School ran a close second because teenage girls can be mean. Girls thought I was stuck up, anti-social, that I actually "high sided" them, as one girl put it. Truth is, I felt lonely, awkward, wanted to belong and fit in, but at the same time wanted to express who I was, whoever that was at the moment. Even at church, where I finally found life friends, where I probably felt the most comfortable and received the greatest support and encouragement, I still felt that the me that everyone thought they knew only scratched the surface. I still felt out of place, like I had to tiptoe into the room, apologize for my presence. I wasn't perfect. I screwed up, but my screw-ups, in comparison to my peers, seemed to echo throughout the stratosphere. There seemed no space in the world that was big enough to include me. These are the feelings that shaped my perception of myself, my world, and my relationship to it.

Not all of my feelings can I associate with any particular experience, but I remember the feelings oh so well. I remember feeling misunderstood, alone, forgotten, rejected, insignificant. I remember feeling that there was more to me than people could see, and if only they could see it, they would accept me, wholly, completely. Yet, I didn't know how to just be me, either.

There will be many who will say, "No, it wasn't that way at all. How could she say that? Is she being dramatic? Why is she making this shit up?" Outwardly, appearances can tell a different tale, but it has become important to me that I speak of what was going on inside of me, understand how it got there, why it remained for so long, but more importantly, discover what it was trying to say. In fact, let me say here and now, that should these words become the stuff of books, and should there be others than myself who read them and come to learn the language of feelings, it is my choice to stand naked and vulnerable. I might lose friends, clients, and even the respect of those who are keepers of the past, but it won't kill me. I intend to come out more alive than I've ever been. Unfortunately, "no man is an island unto himself"; our paths cross with others. I recognize that not everyone is ready to bare their skins, and I respect that, but, again, this is something I must do to heal myself. So, I pause here to offer a word:

DISCLAIMER

It is not my intent to blame, discredit, humiliate, slander, vilify, or castigate anyone mentioned or alluded to in my memoirs, nor is there an intent to tarnish the reputation of anyone mentioned or alluded to in these recollections. These are my memories, from my perspective, which may be remembered differently by others. In most cases, names have been omitted. Names of children from my childhood have been changed to respect their innocence. In other cases, if anyone knows me at all, it will be obvious about whom I am speaking. Regardless, in such instances, names have been omitted; where names are mentioned, it is because there is no negative situation tied to the individual, or the individual has given me permission to do so. For those who are deceased, it is not my intent to dishonor their memory, but, again, these are my memories of my experiences, from my perspective, intended only to help me understand and work through the feelings they engendered, which have remained with me throughout my life, impacted my perception of myself, my world, and my relationship to it.

I realize my life has probably been a cake walk compared to some, and believe it or not, I am grateful for what it has been. I finally have no regrets; okay, maybe one or two. Every step I have made has brought me to where I AM and who I AM. Nope, there was no molestation or physical abuse as a child; my father didn't run off and leave the family – not to work on the railroad or the chain gang, not to start a second family, neither to find himself nor lose himself. He was there, being Daddy as best he knew how. I have no half siblings. In fact, I have had the best three sisters and one step-sister in the world. As siblings we had and have our stuff; as a step-sibling there has been some stuff. Two are deceased and there are two quite insane ones left with me, Pam and Joby; we are as different as night and day, but I would not trade them. While I smoked my share of weed prior to 1987 (things changed in 1987), and drank my share of spirits, still do, there is not nor has there ever been any addiction in my life. There have been no debilitating illnesses or health challenges that I have conquered courageously. I've never even been in the hospital, except to give birth to my daughter, who was born healthy and strong, and, except for strep throat and a few rotten teeth, has been healthy and strong ever since. So, for some, maybe many, my preoccupation with the feelings I have carried with me throughout my life might seem trite, or petty, and that's a problem. In fact, it's THE problem.

In this society, if our experiences aren't BREAKING NEWS, fodder for a TMZ expose', Facebook tea, Twitter gossip, or inspiration for a new hash tag, they are nothing.

Yet, the average person walking around today has had experiences that have greatly impacted his personal life, leaving behind feelings he or she has never examined, never considered as the source of all the discord, issues, and challenges plaguing his daily existence. Few realize that understanding those feelings could change the total trajectory of their lives. I like to say that if we can make sense of our lives, we can make our lives make sense. Depression is claiming so many; imagine how many could be saved if they just knew that the answer is not to rid themselves of what they feel, but explore those feelings, go into them, get into them. Instead, we are told that our issues are nothing. If they are not earth shattering we are told to suck it up or let it go. So, we don't get to feel through our experiences, and we miss out on what they have come to tell us.

Children cry, and we say, "Stop crying, or I'll give you something to cry about" – as if what he or she is crying about isn't already enough. So, they stop crying. They are no longer sad (emotion), but who knows what residue (feeling) this experience has left behind. Children get angry and pout, and we say, "Fix your face." So, they fix their faces, then what? It doesn't change how they feel; it probably exacerbates it. What if we could teach children when they are young to ask themselves: "What do I feel? What has caused me to feel this way? How would I rather feel? So, what is this feeling telling me? Now what should I do with this information?" What if we could teach them that no experience is wasted, nor the feelings left behind?

What if every adult could do that for herself/himself?

Looking my dreams in the face, knowing they were right within reach, refusing to come up empty handed, I became fully aware that everything I had done in my life could all end up for naught. A lot of compromises had already been made; I had often felt like a prisoner in a prison of my own creation, attracting, meditating, vibrating by default, knowing full well that the essence, the fullness of who I AM was just within my grasp. I decided it was time to figure out what was really going on here. The common denominator I found were the feelings I held about myself, and I had the good sense to know it was time to explore what I was feeling inside.

Learning the language of feelings,
… my sanity depended on it.
… moving forward in my life required it.
… answering my life question demanded it.
… my Spirit compelled it.
… embracing who I AM prerequisite it.

The more I discounted my feelings, the more I accused my own self of being overly dramatic, saying to myself, "Girl, that ain't nothin', least you're alive, healthy, got a job; be thankful", the more those feelings wreaked havoc in my life. I decided I wanted to make my life make sense.
At a deeper level, in what I call the Soul Space, I knew there was something that my Soul had come here to be and do and have and say, etc., etc., etc. I believed that getting to

the core of those deeply held feelings would shed light on that as well, and connect me with who I AM. My life was calling me to action. I had to answer. My life mattered.
I ultimately decided that I was worth the time and energy. In the words of Miss Celie in *The Color Purple*,

> "I'm poor, black; I may even be ugly.
> But dear God! I'm here! I'm here!"

Thank You Nuh Nuh

"NuhNuh! NuhNuh!"

I had moved into my family's original home, a little wood frame down at the very end of Hanfro Street in Acres Homes – Houston, Texas, bordered on two sides by the graveyard, the same graveyard where my mama was buried. I had done a little work on the house and thought it a pretty quaint place to live for a minute. There was more work to do, but I had gotten started; my sister's god father built new cabinets and installed them in the kitchen; I laid down a new floor myself, cheap carpet on top; changed out some bathroom plumbing. I had worked at Finger's Furniture up to my graduation from UH and had furnished my first apartment; so, I was good on furniture. One of my best friends, Sharon, had moved in with me for a while, but I guess it wasn't her cup of tea. So, she soon moved out, and young, single mom and daughter were gonna make a go of it, our first time living alone. I had no idea my older sister, Joby, would decide that I didn't need to live behind a grave yard by myself and move in, but good thing she did as she helped scare off a would-be burglar one night. Negro from across the street, we had known the family from way back, tried to crawl in through the kitchen window!

So, there I was, checking the mail, and I hear a woman's voice, calling. "NuhNuh! NuhNuh!

I looked around, seeing no one at first, wondering who the heck was calling, "NuhNuh! NuhNuh!" and who the hell was NuhNuh. From what I could see, I was the only person down there, on that dead end, gravel road. Finally, a slender figure made its way around an over-hanging tree.

"NuhNuh! You know I'm talking to you girl. You know we used to call you NuhNuh."

"Nope", I thought to myself, "I didn't", and when she finally got close enough, I told her so. I did recognize her as an old family friend, Ms. Ora. We embraced and I shared that I had no idea that was my nickname for a minute. As she chatted on, asking about the well-being of everybody in the family, name by name, some names I had to provide after deciphering who she could possibly be talking about, my mind flashed back to third grade. My teacher was talking about nicknames, and was going down each row asking kids if they had a nickname. One boy's nickname was Man. Linda's nickname was Penny. There was a Chelle, and a couple of Juniors in the room, and I would bet money there was a Bubbah. I had no nickname, not like the others anyway. Norm just didn't seem to be a real nickname, and I dared not reveal that my father often called me String Bean and Pork Bone because I was so skinny; I just didn't need that kind of attention in my life; so, I made one up. Ms. Ora went on about how the street had changed, the community had changed, Black people had changed, and not for the better. I thought to myself that had I remembered being called NuhNuh, I might have shared that with my oh, so obnoxious third grade teacher; but, in the absence of a real nickname, I just lied.

I remember the NuhNuh story like it was yesterday. It would be years before I would understand why it remained with me. My sister, Joby, has helped keep it alive through the years, retelling it and laughing as if she were there herself. However, it would be years before I would find the symbolism in it. In my head, I was moving into my dad's rental property, which happened to be the house where I was born, to start anew and get my footing, to save some money and lay a foundation for myself and my daughter, but my Spirit was taking me back to my beginning. Life was saying, begin at the beginning. While I was physically on one quest, I was, spiritually, on another. Yet, the two were running parallel, trying to align, calling me back, requiring that I go back to my beginning. Nuh Nuh was that beginning; she had been there through it all. She knew where all the bodies were buried ... figuratively.

I found Nuh Nuh that day at the mailbox; like a postcard from my subconscious, she "entered my consciousness, and stayed there" (words borrowed from Lorraine Hansberry; they come to me a lot. I'll explain why later on). Still, it would be many years before I realized what she had come to say. It would be years before I discovered that I was actually on a quest that day at the mailbox, and not until this moment, would I discover that my search for belonging, acceptance, significance, the fullness of myself, for home, for the smell of garlic on Sunday could have ended, right there.

So, rather than lump you in the acknowledgements, I want to say, Thank you, NuhNuh. Thank you for being there, for being all that you have been through the years, for being the girl who introduced me to the woman I AM, the bullied, the motherless, the friendless, the unworthy, the scorned, the slow drag girl, the she dog in heat, the invisible, the single mom, the divine manifestation. I offer you, in gratitude for this journey…
THE SMELL OF GARLIC ON SUNDAY

PROLOGUE

Every master was once a disaster.

T. Harv Ecker

All in My Feelings

I had been asked to produce a show at my church for the 2014 Holy Season (Thanksgiving, Ramsa Moja, Advent, Hanukkah, Christmas, and Kwanza). It was immediately something I believed in, something I thought the community could use. If you recall, being African American in 2014 was no picnic. It was the year of Ferguson, MO, everything that set it off, and everything that came out of it, good, bad, and indifferent. The plea for the world to acknowledge that *Black Lives Matter* was embraced all over the world by average, ordinary people; yet, here in America, that effort on behalf of the Black community was snatched up and rendered racist and exclusive, dismissive of the exclusivity of the most recent overt injustices, and replaced with *All Lives Matter.* The justice system was not on our side. Federal, State, and Local government seemed to have turned a deaf ear and blind eye to all that was going on. In fact, internationally, governments of the free world seemed hell bent on ridding itself of descendants of Africans. That's no conspiracy theory; I've got a push pin graph of international incidents regarding people of color to prove it. In my estimation, the community needed hope. So, I wanted this project to be a message of hope, received by many. Out of it was the possibility for a comprehensive, well thought out, well planned program to take shape in Houston as part of the Black Lives Matter Movement. I wanted it to be a grand success.

When I submitted to the sponsoring organization what it would take to mount this production, it appeared to be more than they wanted to take on. In that moment, I could see no other way of doing this particular project, at least, in the manner it had been presented to me and was now stuck in my head. Additionally, as usual, time was of the essence; there was not a lot of time for going back to the drawing board. So, I proposed that, if they would provide the financing that was comfortable to them, that they were already prepared to invest, which would simply cover the cost of opening the doors to our main sanctuary, and help bring it to fruition, promoting it in the manner they had determined when they birthed the idea, I would take the helm of the project. They agreed; then, they disappeared. I mean no insult or embarrassment to any who may be reading these words, but, in truth, that's what happened. They backed out of the effort to make the event all that it could be. The sister who initially met with me, and one other stayed the course as best they could. Shout out to Dalilah (Geynille Agee) and Theuda (Elandis Cashe)!
I called together another small team to take the helm of the Black Lives Matter element of the project as well as to help with the promotions; it was a free show and if marketed and promoted well should attract a healthy segment of the community. As I checked in weekly with the team; nothing much was happening. Though I had produced numerous

shows prior to this one with even greater budgets, in professional houses, I felt I needed to go inward to gather all the power and energy I would need to make sure this project fulfilled its objective. To me, it seemed like such a great community outreach opportunity, something that we, as a church, should be doing, offering "a message of hope to a community in crisis". Once into the process, I wondered frequently if I had been wrong. Maybe I should have taken the time to go back to the drawing board and created something that others could wrap their minds, hearts, and energy around and fully embrace. The journey kept telling me otherwise.

I meditate every day, but for the production period, I increased my meditation time and frequency. I journal regularly, but for this endeavor, I journaled twice, daily, in the morning and at night. I read inspirational works all the time, but I made doubly sure there was something on hand during this period, and I would read before turning in at night, after scrolling through Facebook, of course. It was in my reading, I'm not sure which source, that I came across the topic of removing blocks to success by disclosing and uprooting limiting beliefs. It wasn't a new topic and what it suggested wasn't new; it just struck a new chord within me. It suggested using the "Life Review" as a process of identifying those limiting beliefs.

If you're a dreamer, a visionary, have goals and aspirations that you're trying to realize, or if you're simply trying your damnedest to be a better person, you might have already discovered that the road to your destination is not as smooth or straight as you had initially imagined. You, more than once, have probably felt the need to stop and look back over your path to gain clarity about where you're trying to go, understand why you desire to go there, assess the journey you have made thus far, and determine if the direction and the destination are even right for you. You've probably stopped in your tracks and yelled, "WTF?!" Like I, you probably have reviewed every "mistake" you've ever made, analyzed every "failure", re-enacted every "bad decision". You probably, like I on many occasions, have looked back over your life to find where you were taught and embraced limiting beliefs and self-sabotaging behaviors, and sought to clear them out. As I, you have probably gone all the way back to your childhood to exorcise those proverbial demons. Been there; done that, but there must be something I missed. This project was worth another trip back down memory lane, without the soulful sounds of Minnie Ripperton playing in the background, however.

Embarking upon this "Life Review", it occurred to me that I could remember some things like they happened yesterday, while there were other things my sisters or my father might mention that I had no recollection of. I realized that those incidents I remembered most clearly were those that were emotionally charged, negative or positive. Then there were those with emotional residue attached to them, feelings, deep feelings I couldn't seem to shake, feelings that, when called by name, sent pains into my shins, literally. As clearly as I remembered certain events, I remembered how I felt. In fact, the feelings I was left with, from past experiences, were often clearer than the details of the experiences themselves. As I spent some time with awareness, some feelings I thought I had dealt with and laid to rest resurfaced, propelling me to ask. "Why is this feeling so damned strong? Why won't it go away?" It was on this occasion that I realized my feelings were speaking and I needed to learn their language. Now, there is a great possibility that with all the self - help stuff out there, someone has already come to this revelation. Well, it was an ah-ha moment for me; so, I went with it. I even started what I called a Feelings Journal.

At this point in my life, consciously and consistently going inward for guidance and awareness was a daily practice. I had wrestled often with my personal issues; I had looked my "demons" in the face and called them by name. More times than I can count, I had sat with, visited, and shared pots of coffee with my feelings of inadequacy and worthlessness. By then, I had entertained, with song, dance and drama, my feelings of being unwelcomed, uninvited, unaccepted, weird, different, and out of place. I'd read books and written poems about the fear of rejection. I was not afraid of introspection. I welcomed it. Yet, never had I thought to ask, "What have these feelings come to say?" Experiences, yes; feelings, no. I knew that every experience served a purpose, and by the time I began this feelings journey, I had already made it a habit to examine every experience for how it served my life's purpose or spiritual growth. But what was I supposed to do with the feelings that lingered? I had never thought to ask. I recognized that this exercise was about to be the pièce de résistance of self - awareness and actualization. This would be the stuff of quantum leaps. I decided to go with this *Feelings* epiphany, turn inward of myself, cleanse myself of all limitations, and with a six-week no-sugar fast, produce this Holy Season show like a beast!

In my Feelings Journal, I decided to write down every experience that would come to me, as far back as I could remember, about which I still held strong feelings. I went all the way back to my childhood, back to incidents that I knew still gave me an emotional charge. I jotted down things I had written about in plays and short stories, that had become topics of poems in an effort to purge and heal, those things that still drew tears, not for myself, the now me, but the me who had endured each experience, for NuhNuh, and the other me's that had emerged over the years. Where there was no longer an emotional charge to some memories, there were lingering feelings about them, and I had to write them down, feel them, hear what they had to say. As the kids say, I was "all in my feelings".

During this time, my step-mother was in hospice; she had been there since late October. Her long battle with the debilitating effects of the diabetes mind game was slowly being lost. So, the writing was also an effort to clear away the debris of a ragged relationship that had been dropping loose threads in my life since I was 10 years old. I knew some of those threads were getting tangled in the engine of my being, so to speak, blocking me, prohibiting my movement forward. I not only wanted the production to be a success, I wanted to seize the opportunity to clear all the blocks that had kept my dreams and life visions at bay, and I knew the relationship with my step-mother was a big piece of that.

Besides, I was ashamed of myself. During my step-mother's illness, prior to the long hospital stay and ultimate hospice, I would often go to my parents' house to clean and cook. She was so mean and ornery; I originally said that I was doing it for my Dad, not her. He was in his late 80's, had his hands full with her, had his own ailments and couldn't do some things he once could, and was still working every day. I just wanted him to have some relief and eat well, live in a comfortable space, and enjoy his golden years. Then, one day, she made the statement to my sister, "Norm just come and do what she gon' do and leave; she don't say much of nothing." I was ashamed of myself. I realized that no matter how she had made me feel my entire life, and no matter how the illness brought out more of her true nature, I was not the person who would make another feel insignificant. So, I began to sit and chat a few minutes before jumping into the tasks to be done. In my defense, I was going to my parents' house after work, after 5pm. Grocery shopping had become erratic; so, I most always stopped by the store to grab something to cook. Because of my mother's illness and thanks to their little untrained dog, there was always lots to do to keep the house clean and sanitary. Knowing I would be exhausted when I left there, still needing to get home and cook my own dinner and prepare for work the next day, I really wanted to jump into it and get it done.

I was in the kitchen one day, and after playing 20 questions about what I was cooking and why neither she nor my dad were going to eat it, I looked through the window of the bar and caught a glimpse of my step-mother, the woman who had become my mother at the age of ten, but was never really a mother. What I saw was a broken child who had never healed, and I felt sorry for her. I wondered what had happened in her life experiences, what emotional residue was still holding her hostage. I knew that the person who had injured me as a child, a teen, and young adult, who I, only a few years before, had stopped in her tracks from trying to injure me as an almost middle-aged woman, was just a child whose cry for help was never answered, whose emotions were never released, whose feelings were never explored. I knew there would be no sudden awakening with tears of apology for the damage she had done in my life. I would have to forgive someone who would never ask for it. To a relationship that was clearly nearing its end, I would have to bring my own closure; I would have to put it all into perspective on my own. I looked at my step-mother and did not see her. I saw her Spirit and I felt pity dissipate into a love for her I never knew possible. Getting into my feelings, learning their language had come right on time.

The writing presented itself in short stories and anecdotes sometimes interrupted by sudden thoughts, revelations, and discoveries. Sometimes, I would pause and place these reflections in brackets; periodically, I would stop altogether and assess what I had gained from the memories: awarenesses, new insights, epiphanies, and ah-ha moments; I called them Check-Ins. It was clear from the outset that this was not just about producing a show with a message that many would receive; it wasn't just about removing obstacles to the realization of dreams. Clearing away the pains of my relationship with my step-mother wasn't even at the center of it all.

This was and is about actually seeing the synchronicity and the divine intention in everything I had magnetized into my life via agreement, default, or intention, and understanding the purpose it was intended to serve. I had to get in my feelings to do that!

So, this is about the sharing of one soul's "adventure through the jungle of space and time" (Mike Dooley), and how learning the language of feelings allowed that soul to discover the theme of her adventure and, in turn, remember where she was trying to go, measure everything in life, thereafter, by that destination, inviting every adventurer, every traveler, every sojourner to do the same.

This is a memoir, my recollections of the experiences that spawned the feelings I held about myself, the conclusions I drew as a result of remembering, the questions I raised, the answers that surfaced, and the "Sacred Themes" that emerged.

PART I

Your children are not your children.
They are sons and daughters of Life's longing for itself.
They come through you but not from you.
And though they are with you they belong not to you.

You may give them your love but not your thoughts,
For they have their own thoughts.
You may house their bodies but not their souls,
For their souls dwell in the house of tomorrow, which you
cannot visit, not even in your dreams.

Khalil Gibran

This Ain't No Party

I sat there, quietly observing the activity around me. A boy, I'll call him J, sat across the table from me, just as quiet, just as alone. It was Valentine's Day, I was in Kindergarten, and we were having a party. It didn't feel like a party though.

[Would no one play with me? Or, would I not play with anyone? I wasn't the most talkative child. A friend of my birth-mother's once told me I went a period of time without talking at all. She said they were a little frightened for me for awhile, thought I might be special … funny. I'm wondering, too, would no one play with J? Or, would J not play with anyone?]

Still, there was a party going on, lots of running around, back and forth, except J and me, and there had been lots of punch. So much punch that I guess the trips to the restroom, which was right inside our classroom, were becoming a bit much for our teacher, Mrs. Benjamin. She exclaimed, in no uncertain terms, "No more punch! And not another soul is to go to that restroom!"

Well, we're 5, Mrs. Benjamin; I'm 5, and I'm literal, very literal. In her defense, as I did love Mrs. Benjamin, there might have been a couple of toilet stop-ups, and we might have been sharing the facilities with the adjoining classroom. Still, I had to go, but she had said don't go. So, what do I do? Do I go, or don't go? Both. I don't go, and I go, right there in my chair. Now, not only am I sitting at a table alone, except for J, the quiet boy, while the other kids run around having the time of their lives, I am now the center of frustrated attention as Mrs. Benjamin has a conniption because she has to clean up pee.

[I'm 5. What do I do with that?]

I hang my head and feel like crap, the same thing I do every day in Reading Circle when Mrs. Benjamin seats us all in the exact same spots - me to her right and the book satchel boy to her left - because we can read, and when she gets tired, she can pass her book off to one of us before going around that dreaded, stammering, stumbling circle; at least, that's what my 5 year-old head deduced. It's hard to say what the others thought; I just know that one person didn't like it; I'll call her Bully Girl. I remember her being a very smart girl later in our school years; so, maybe she could read too and wanted equal time. I just know she wanted that seat beside Mrs. Benjamin and she fought for it every day. Every day, she pinched me in my side, on my arm, on my thighs, and hell, that hurt. So, I squirmed, trying to get away from her, and Mrs. Benjamin would pat me on the leg to be still, then a double pat, followed by a furrowed brow, a quiet but stern reprimand between her teeth, "Be still". Then came the stares, giggles, unwanted attention, or rather, the wrong kind of attention. Yet, I never told. I simply endured. Bully Girl fought for what she wanted. She could have found another tactic, got dammit; but, there was a lesson in that; one I would learn many years later. Unfortunately, right now, I'm 5.

[What does one do with that, every day? First, you wonder, why you. You wonder what's "wrong" with you, because, surely, there must be something wrong with you.]

I'm 5 and I think there must be something wrong with me, especially when the party resumes and Mrs. Benjamin has calmed her nerves and explained what she really meant about the no restroom policy, but even if I got up the nerve to get up and join the fun, I can't, because I'm now wet from sitting in my own urine, thinking. This ain't no party.

No More Parties

My Dad was getting me all spiffied up as my sisters watched. It was the time I almost got bopped in the mouth for repeating words I didn't know the meaning of. See we're a family of smart mouths; we get it from both our parents. So Pam said something to Daddy and Daddy responded with something smart-mouthed, and I said,

"Ah ha, he pissed you off".

Pam and Joby laughed. They were always laughing at me; they were a team.

Daddy said, "Where'd you get that from?"

I said, "Paaam."

Pam's smart mouth flew open.

Daddy said. "What does it mean?"

I said, "I'on know".

He tried to bop me in my mouth, but I ducked. Still, I learned that day; don't use words you don't know the meaning of.

I was excited about going to my cousin Sandy's birthday party. I was more excited about going to Big Alice's house. Big Alice was my mother's first cousin on the Wright side of the family. We called her Big Alice because there were three Alice's in the family. It was one of the few times children were allowed to call grown-ups by their first name. Otherwise, we called grown up cousins Aunt and Uncle. Big Alice was hosting Sandy's party; Sandy was her granddaughter. I loved going to Big Alice's house; she was the hostess with the mostest. I loved to watch her entertain. We had lots of family gatherings at her house, and what was a decent wood framed house always appeared extremely large to me. The adults would gather in the front room for coffee, beer, high balls (their name for mixed drinks). If Joby was present, I joined all the kids outside in some game that involved lots of running, or gravitated toward the adult room only to be shooed away. Perhaps, it is how I honed my storytelling skills, as all they did when they gathered was tell a bunch of lies. Now, that's what my daddy used to say, but I almost got bopped in the mouth again for saying the exact same thing.

"Y'all ain't gon' do nothin' but sit around, drinkin', an' tellin' a bunch o' lies."

It was one of those occasions at our own house of gravitating to the adult room. I had just served up sugar and cream to my uncles, Uncle Randle and Uncle Samuel, who I thought were twins named Ram and Sam thanks to our language of choice, Ebonics. They were really my Dad's first cousins once removed, making them my second cousins once removed, but I called them uncle because, again, Black children didn't call adults by their first name in those days. I had served up the cream and sugar, and was being ordered to the back with the children.

"Y'all ain't gon' do nothin' but sit around, drinkin', an' tellin' a bunch o' lies." I innocently pleaded.

My uncles chuckled into their cups. I'm guessing they thought it funny and quite true, but knew that I was totally out of line and did not want to encourage whatever it was that I was exhibiting. My daddy immediately snapped.

"What chu say?"

The literal me answered. I had not yet learned there was such a thing as a rhetorical question, or that type of question intended to force one to think about what she has said or done, not encourage her to repeat it. So, I repeated.

"Y'all ain't gon' do nothin' but sit around, drinkin', an' tellin' a bunch o' lies." .

By then, my uncles' heads were falling backwards, their mouths wide with laughter, each stamping a foot against the floor, slapping one knee. My daddy, recognizing my innocence, and possibly that I was repeating what they all said every time they got together, and a bit tickled himself, explained that it was not proper for children to accuse adults of lying. In fact, children do not say the word lie at all.

So, the adults would gather in the front room of Big Alice's house and take turns telling lies, the next one bigger than the last. I loved the way Big Alice would enter the room and serve up something from the kitchen. She would say a few words and the entire room would go up in laughter! I wanted to be like Big Alice, the person who captured everybody's attention as soon as she walked into the room.

We arrived at Big Alice's and everybody remarked how pretty I looked. Even though I felt pretty, I thought they were all just being nice because my mama had been dead barely a year and they wanted my daddy to know he was doing a good job with four girls. Somewhere between my entry into the front room and my father's questioning glances, something must have come over me. My next memory is that of sitting in a chair by the archway that joined the two sections of the front room; that second section was like a Dining Room. Big Alice served coffee to all the adults who had brought children to the party. She brought me a cup of punch and asked if I was ready to go to the back of the house where the party was. I shook my head no, looking into my daddy's worried eyes. Everybody in the room felt sorry for me. I felt sorry for my daddy; surely, I had to be embarrassing him. I had to get up the nerve to go back there. So, I did. I slid out of my chair and made my way to what seemed to be the longest hallway in the world.

I was met by a little girl who grabbed my hand and said, "Hey! You wanna play a game?"

That must have been the hallway to heaven. I was ecstatic. "Yes!" I squealed, nodding, smiling.

The little girl stepped a little closer to me, looked into my eyes, which were hazel, like nobody else's in the family except my daddy's and my sister's, and said, "Oh, you're not Sandy".

She threw my hand aside and ran away. I stood there for a few seconds, alone, watching that eternal run. I turned and ran back down that long hallway in the opposite direction (think Logan's Run), back to my chair beside the archway. I drank punch. I ate cake. I listened to adult lies. I wondered what the children in the back were doing. I told myself it didn't matter because I was never going to another party again in life.

Well, I lied. At least 8 or 9 years later, I would find myself at the door of a party being thrown by a girl from my church, waiting to be let in, only to be turned away, with no idea why. This girl literally said, "She's not invited to my party."

[What the hell was it with me and parties?]

The Retarded Class
*the names have been changed to protect the innocent

All the smart kids from Kindergarten went to one class, the teachers' kids, the preachers' kids, the kids whose parents headed the PTA, the kids whose parents were active and visible. I was neither. Well, my Dad was visible; he was the bus driver, not a highly respected position. My mom was in and out of the hospital fighting for her life. So, I was placed in Mrs. Willie Lou Brown's first grade class with J, the quiet boy from Kindergarten, and Elizabeth, a little mongoloid girl who had seizures regularly and sent everyone running to the cafeteria for a spoon to hold down her tongue.

[Now, I am fully aware that the appropriate terminology is Downs Syndrome, but we didn't know that then, and I must remain firmly planted in that space and time, go into the head of that 6 year old in order to relive her experience, feel her feelings. As well, I am fully aware that the acceptable terms today are Learning Challenged, Academically Challenged, Special Needs, ADD and the like, not "retarded", but it's 1965.]

In this class, there was Janice, who was "retarded" and wild as hell; no one could control her. She would just get up and run out of class, round and round the courtyard. All of the main classrooms at Highland Heights Elementary, and the Cafeteria, opened to the courtyard then; so, you could see Janice running around, peeping into other classes, speaking to all the teachers, making a whole lot of noise. It was really pretty comical to watch, but we were taught that you don't laugh at retarded kids; you feel sorry for them; so, I didn't allow myself to laugh. But why the hell would I feel sorry for Janice? I envied Janice. While I didn't necessarily want to run around the courtyard or peep into other classes, I, very often, wanted to get up and run out of the classroom with her, out of the building, and far, far away. Then, there was the girl who smelled like bacon grease, but was really pretty sharp; so, I wondered why she was in the retarded class. Big Eyed S was the girl who lied on me, daily.

[In my six year-old brain, this was the retarded class, and I was in it. What does a 6 year old do with that? How would this make a clearly alert 6 year old feel?

Answer: She defines herself, and grows increasingly at odds with the soft voice inside telling her that she is not retarded, that she is more than she thinks she is, more than she sees in the mirror, and far more than what everybody else obviously sees. She even writes her own songs about how special she is. Unfortunately, she does not know that the human brain is wired for survival; so, by default, she picks up the negative impulses, thoughts, and feelings far more quickly than the positive so that she prepared to defend herself. By default, she ignores that soft voice.

[45]

Thus, sitting in the Retarded Class, she feels betrayed.]

Didn't Mrs. Benjamin tell the Principal I was one of the top readers in the class?

[She doesn't realize that not being very talkative often signals to the unenlightened that one is incapable of communication and obviously, slow, retarded even. She hasn't been introduced to the term "introvert"; so, it has no bearing on her understanding that there is nothing wrong with being a loner; so, she desires friends for all the wrong reasons. Bottom line, in her little brain, she reasons that she just wasn't smart enough and her parents weren't special enough for her to be in Mrs. Treadville's class.

Her 6 year old voice whispers, "There's nothing wrong with you; it's them. They don't even have sense enough to keep a couple of spoons in the classroom and they know Elizabeth is going to have another seizure. So, how do they know who's retarded and who's not?" But she believes what she sees, begins an adversarial relationship with that little voice, and is on track to argue with it for the rest of her life. She's in the retarded class and her only way out is to prove that she's smart. The only way to be treated special, to be worthy of anything is to be smart. Being smart gets you seated next to the teacher. Being smart gets you in the class with kids who dress better than you, who don't run wild or have seizures, smell like bacon, or lie on you. So, smart it would be.

They say that a child's personality is formed by the age of six. By that age, the ego, the persona that a child presents to the world as a defense mechanism, when she's no longer a toddler and nobody comes running when she cries, is firmly in place. Well, life set me up, and by the age of six, I was a survivor, competitive, and determined, despite the odds against me.]

I had to get out of that class, and the very teacher who didn't seem to have sense enough to realize that a kid who says nothing all day every day is not likely to suddenly start jabbering as soon as the teacher leaves the room and have her name placed at the top of the Talkers List, every day, by the same name-taker, every day, and get spanked for it, every day, gave me the clue as to exactly what I needed to do. This teacher had whispered to the 2nd grade teacher next door as they stood between the adjoining doors, gossiping. "She's a smart little girl", she said. "She doesn't belong in here." I overheard. Smart, that was it. I had to be smart and everybody had to know it.

Confirmation came when I found myself sitting in that same gossiping teacher's 2nd grade class, with kids I had been separated from the year before, and out-scored them on everything. It was confirmed when I spoke better than they did on the school program, and everybody said so. It was confirmed when they all suddenly became my childhood friends.

My Mama Died Last Night

… is what I told my first grade teacher, Mrs. Willie Lou Brown. I really liked Mrs. Willie Lou (pronounced Miss-Wi-Lou). She missed the mark a lot of times though, the spoon for Elizabeth, the Talkers' List. She spanked me every day because her name-taker, Big Eyed S, I secretly called her, wrote my name down on the Talkers' List every time Mrs. Willie Lou left the room, but at least she knew I was not retarded and did not belong in her classroom.

When I got to school the morning after Daddy had walked into his bedroom, where we had all fallen asleep, Kathy, Pam, Joby, and I, and gave us the news, "She's gone", that was the first thing I told her. She said, "I know, baby, I know", and even helped me take my jacket off. She had never helped me take my jacket off before. Velma Joyce Westmoreland Thomas had died of cirrhosis of the liver. I had no idea what that was; so, I had no idea that everyone would think my mama was an alcoholic. I got that question a lot as a young adult, when asked how my mother died. "Was she alcoholic?" Imagine if my 6 year old brain had to deal with that.

[I remember so many times, longing for my mother, wanting her with me so badly, while at the same time, feeling like I barely knew her. I remember this crazy woman whipping me because I wouldn't move out the way of a firecracker. The idiots who threw the firecracker, two boys from the neighborhood who had no business crossing through my backyard anyway, got off scot-free. When I ran in the house yelling that Cookie or Baines, I forget which one it was, and one of their friends had thrown a firecracker at the back of my foot, I just knew she'd be out that front door and across the street to their grandmother, seeing to it that they got the paddling of their lives. Oh to the contrary, Velma Joyce Westmoreland Thomas asked me why I didn't move when they told me to move. My question to her was, "Shouldn't they have thrown the firecracker in the other direction, not toward me?" Then I finished with my infamous conclusion. "Well then." A friend of the family actually called me Well Then. We called him Papa Chief, a handsome, blue-black cowboy named Isadore Wycoff. He taught us how to ride horses. He would always say, when I entered the room, "Here comes ol' Well Then. What chu up to, Well Then?" So, it might have been the "well then" that did it, because my mama went right ahead and whipped me for not getting out of the way.

The firecracker incident, washing my hair in her beauty shop, and popping my hands every time I rolled my skirt up to my panties, a nervous twitch that took over me while singing a solo in church, are all the memories I have of my mama; there may be one or two others out of reach at this moment, but they aren't many. It would take me a lifetime to realize that she and I had made an agreement. I would be born to her, but she would not hang around to give me the

love of a mother, the unparalleled, unequalled, unconditional, irreplaceable mother's love. We agreed, before sojourning to this land, that her absence would send me in search of that love, and everything it stood for.
The fact that my mother put me on program to sing when I was 4, lets me know that she saw something in me. I'm not a great singer, but I can carry a tune. I hear music very well, which is odd. I actually compose, but I love to perform. Remembering that time she simply hunched my father and laughed as I pulled my white blouse from inside my blue skirt, fresh from Night Church, held my soda bottle from the lip as I swigged and pimp walked around my uncle's pool table, my cue stick hitting the floor with every other step, lets me know - she got me! (I caught their eyes, my mom laughing, my dad shaking his head. My memory. Intentionally planted, for me, for just this moment. Thank you, Mama.)

Throughout my life, I would need somebody to "get me", but we had agreed; she would not be there to do it. She knew who I was already, an artist with a well-balanced yin and yang, but we had agreed, the one person who would have accepted me without judgement and loved me anyway would leave me early on. If she had not been sick, she would have realized I was in the Retarded Class and she would have gotten me out, but my being there was serving a higher purpose. So, we agreed; she would not be there to save me. We knew, while standing at the portal of life, that the aloneness and helplessness I would feel while being bullied, the alienation I would feel as a small child, the insignificance, and yes, the feeling of motherlessness would fuel the quest that was to define my life question and my soul's journey. The rest of my life, I would search for the smell of garlic on Sunday with a vengeance.]

Of course, I didn't know anything about cirrhosis of the liver; so, I shared the news of Mama's passing with Miss Wi-Lou as only a six year-old in a Retarded Class could.

Smart is All I Got

"She think she smart. She think she something. Why you talk white?"

[In the favorite words of my granddaughter, Leelah, "Come ooon!"

Leelah Imani-Afua Washington, my mini-me, pictured here only because her sister was included in the Introduction. God forbid I include one and not the other.

I mean, really? I had just discovered my trump card, and and somebody went and changed the game.]

Being smart had been my ticket into elementary school society; first and foremost, it bought my passage out of the Retarded Class, (don't forget I explained my use of the term "retarded" a few pages back). It bought me a few friends, and even assuaged my fear that everybody was always looking at my dingy socks that would never get white again because the vaseline on my legs and patent leather shoes kept attracting all the dirt around. I was smart; so, nobody would be looking at my socks any more. I had gotten this smart thing down pat.

I had made it without incident through 2nd grade, except that time I stretched the truth a little. Then my 3rd grade teacher introduced me to the reality of Black Classism. She was ugly and rude. She had stood in the adjoining doorway with the 5th grade teacher, gossiping about my 2nd grade teacher, who had taken an interest in my father, the school bus driver. Black teachers made house calls in those days; so, it escaped me that she, my 2nd grade teacher, had come to our house to report to my father on my ability to craft very convincing stories, on a Sunday, in the middle of Lawrence Welk for God's sake. I didn't exactly make up the story about traveling to California with my sister; I just changed the dates and added a few characters along the way to make it interesting. I was smart, a straight A student; that didn't warrant a home visit, but Lawrence Welk was on; so, I didn't have time to give it much thought.

"What's wrong with that woman?" I heard my 3rd grade teacher say to her co-gossiper. "What's she going to do with that poor bus driver and his children?"

"Poor bus driver and his children? Bitch! We ain't poor.

You live in one two-story house in 3rd Ward! My daddy owns houses all over Acres Homes, and he runs several businesses."

Of course, I didn't say that. I wanted to say something, but we were taught in those days to respect our teachers, even the ugly ones. Besides, I didn't think of any such retort until many years later, but that pretty much sums up how I felt. Needless to say, I hated my 3rd grade teacher and found other ways to rebel against her snobbery. Plus, being smart had privileges that she could not deny me. Or, so I thought.

I was certain that having my poem, "Summer", published in the Red Cross Magazine, and getting a letter from President L.B. Johnson to congratulate me would secure me a lifetime of friends, cafeteria seats, and oohs and aahs from all my teachers. Yet, I suddenly found myself scared to death to raise my hand and tell this 4th grade teacher that the root of the word "natural" is nature, while these idiots around me are yelling out everything under the sun, and getting pretty creative, I might add. So, maybe I can yell it out there and nobody will know who said it.

"Nature!"

"Who said that?"

All fingers pointed at me, ducking behind the person in front of me, the girl who smelled like bacon grease in 1st grade, and still did, here in 4th grade. Then, as if I were an answered prayer, Mrs. Holloway let out a deep sigh.

"Thank you. The root word is nature."

Then she smiled at me. She didn't patronize me; she didn't spank me; she didn't feel sorry for me; she just frickin' smiled. The same teacher who read my published poem, aloud, the same teacher who read my letter from the President, aloud, the same teacher who whispered to my soon to be step-mother as we drove her home, as if I couldn't hear right behind her in the back seat, "She's the only person in the class who passed the test with a 100", the same teacher who must have looked inside my soul and knew I needed to hear the words, "It's okay to be smart", smiled at me.

[October, 2004, I was presenting a segment of my original, episodic production, *Church Anniversary*, and I was told that Mrs. Holloway had passed. That night, I dedicated the show to her. I think she would have been proud to have been my teacher.]

But, obviously, being smart was not enough. Who are those kids in the cafeteria getting violin lessons? I wondered. Where does one get a violin? I'd like to play violin. My daddy will get me a violin if you tell him to. How come I wasn't included? When God and Mrs. Oliver, my 5th grade teacher, saw fit to send me on an errand to the Office which would require that I pass by the Cafeteria just in time to witness the private lesson taking place, I literally froze in my tracks. I could not move my feet, but my 10yr old brain was still going a mile a minute. I had been introduced to Black Classism, courtesy of my 3rd grade teacher; so, as my eyes panned the circle of kids, it was crystal clear why I was not taking violin lessons. Those violins seemed to speak to me, but I was not allowed to answer. Like star-crossed lovers, we were separated by a glass and discrimination at the hands of my own people. My heart sank. I didn't bounce my way to the Office as I normally would, happy to be selected to run an errand for the teacher, so proud to have a get out of class free card, if even for a few minutes. I was crushed. Transporting an important message to the Office paled in comparison to the thought of hugging a violin. So, I deduced; if being smart can't get you real friends who won't ridicule you for being smart and talking white, the latter of which made no sense given none of us knew any white people, can't help a teacher see past your economic status to how you make her look good as a teacher as ugly as she is, can't get you violin lessons, or a complete brownie uniform [probably unrelated, but I was 10], what good is it? If being smart does not open every door that seems closed to a little 10 year old Black girl, then what good is it?

By the tender age of 11, I would learn that it's no good, and somebody would have my 6th grade award to prove it. Shit! Being smart was all I had, and it turned out, it wasn't worth a damn.

Norma Jo, Meet Racism

I thought I was catching it enough in my little world. Ha! Norma Jo, "your world is about to get a whole lot bigger" (©Walking Dead). Norma Jo, meet racism.

When zoning was announced, I had the opportunity to transfer to Garden Oaks Elementary or Wesley Elementary. Wesley was still predominantly Black; Garden Oaks had no Black children. My eldest sister, Kathy, tried to tell me how great it would be to be the only Black kid in the school; she said I'd probably be on the news and everything. Perhaps, she was thinking I would be the next Ruby Bridges. I wasn't going for it; I had enough issues of my own. There was no way I could stand up for the whole race. I chose Mable B. Wesley, only to be re-zoned and sent back to Highland Heights where I had come from, before the school year ended. It was the first time we would have white teachers, a white Principal, and 4 white kids on our grade level, two boys, two girls. My thought, well, if all else fails, they'll each have a friend. I was 11, and still had friend issues. I later wondered if they had set it up like that on every grade level.

I had struggled with Math earlier in the year, but was able to pull out an A. All I needed was an A in Geography, and that sixth grade award was mine. I did my report on Augusta, Maine, replete with visual aids. My teacher had declared that project was an A+! I could not wait for Awards Day.

Awards Day came, but there would be no dressing up in white dresses and black patent leather shoes. There would be no sixth grade play, and I had secretly promised myself, while watching my sister Joby in her play the year before and determining that it was neither well produced nor well acted, that I would definitely get the lead in my 6th grade play. It was not going to happen. There would be no donuts and coffee for parents either, no songs from the choir. The tradition of the 6th Grade Graduation had been snatched from us without even a blink.

That day, close to the last day of school, the sixth graders were called into the Cafeteria. By now, one of the four white kids who had come to our school was gone. She had been gone the entire last grading period to Oklahoma to help her mom attend to her grandmother. So, one would understand my utter shock and dismay when the winner of the 6th grade award is announced, and all my classmates who had been with me since Kindergarten are pointing at me, knowing it would be me, but the name we hear is The Absent White Girl. She was not present. She had not been present for weeks. Was she even still a student? Could somebody explain how this works? I had straight A's, had made straight A's since Kindergarten. Where was my award?

[I shared this story in an Education class at University of

Houston; oddly enough, there was a woman in the classroom who actually knew the white kids that had been sent to our school; she even knew the Absent White Girl's situation. So, she fully believed my take on the award story. It was nice to finally be believed.

I wrote a narrative many years later in an effort to address my first experience with racism and the feelings it left me with. In that narrative, as the winner of the 6th Grade Award was being announced, I held a monkey eraser in my hand, the kind that might come out of a cereal box, cracker jacks, or bubble gum machine. Though, in real life, we were all friendly to the four white kids and had welcomed them into our school in much the same way the Native Americans had welcomed the Europeans, I added into the narrative that one of my life-long classmates had become embarrassingly attached to the white kids. In my fictional account, I wrote that she stood up and clapped for the Absent winner of the 6th grade award, clapped wildly, going way overboard; so, I threw my monkey eraser and hit her with it, resulting in loss of participation in Free Day for the sixth graders. I needed retribution, and that's how I got it. I wrote a story, put a monkey eraser in my hand, hurled it at my friend instead of the real perpetrators of my betrayal, and called the story "Free Day for DuBois".
I wrote that story to address my feelings about white people and racism, but the deepest feelings, the ones that lingered and shaped my perception of myself, came not from that part of the story.

I had met racism, but it had not affected me in the manner that the incident which followed would. I guess it was easy to process. It was our existence. Though white people were not a part of our immediate lives, we were well aware of the racism that would ensue once they showed up. Segregation was our reality and, as children, integration wasn't a dream come true. In fact, it was King's dream, not ours, but surely he knew best.

The racism and discrimination I had experienced before, especially in Louisiana, had been a way of life. Swimming in separate municipal pools, entering the bus station through the back door, entering the movie theatre through the fire escape and watching movies from the balcony, being prohibited from shopping malls, stopping alongside the highway to pee because we couldn't stop at certain gas stations while traveling was all a way of life; it was what we experienced every day as a people. This, however, was personal. I was now to learn that neither in my little, Black microcosm, nor in the de-segregated macrocosm into which I had been thrust without my permission, did being smart really matter. So, I'm guessing, that's one reason the incident itself did not necessarily leave a scar; it left an awareness. It was what followed that left the scar.]

After school that day, I marched around the corner to my sisters' school where my step-mother would pick us up. I was crying, angry. Some of the very kids who had just last year taunted me for thinking I was smart, did their 11yr-old best to console me. We stopped off at Antioch Baptist

Church on Beall Street where many of us worshipped. The front door of the church was always open, and there was a water fountain as soon as you entered. They patted me on the back as I drank from the fountain.

[The symbolism of it all is just now occurring to me. After my first personal encounter with racism, my first consolation would come at the availability of a Black water fountain. It was there; it was ours; they couldn't take it away. The very thing Black people had fought to eradicate, separate facilities, COLORED drinking fountains, was the very thing that replenished our little spirits. What a price we paid for integration.]

As soon as my sisters and I were picked up, I immediately rattled off my experience, hoping there would be a little indignation on my behalf, the promise of a visit, a letter, a note to the Principal inquiring into the situation.

"Maybe the other girl was smarter, Norm. Maybe you weren't supposed to get the award."

If you can't say anything else about my step-mother, you can say she was consistent. How did I not know that would be her response? My father had, at the beginning of this school year, a month after their marriage, turned over all issues regarding education to my step-mother, considering she was an educator and all, with a Master's degree. Surely, she knew better than he how to handle such incidents. So, that was that. I settled into the back seat for the ride home. I might as well have been in the back of a hearse; all that I was and had ever hoped to be had just died, killed not by racism, but the declaration that The Absent White Girl was probably smarter than I.

[Because the current examination of these two incidents has put them in such close proximity, I can't help but equate my birth mother not taking up for me in the firecracker incident to my step-mother not defending me in the award incident. Motherless child must fight for herself, stand up for herself, obviously a theme of my life, if not the central theme. Perhaps, my step-mother and I also had an agreement. Interesting.]

"Well damn!" Is what I would have said were the year 2016 and I chose to resort to the quips of the day for recourse, but it wasn't. It was 1970, and I had just had my first real experience with racism and what I would later learn to be The Declaration of Black Inferiority and the Acceptance of the Myth of Black Inferiority. It had come and put the last nail in the proverbial coffin, burying my trump card once and for all. I had played the smart card for five years; though it had begun to lose its impact about year three or four, dying a slow death, it was all I had.

Don't Get Me Wrong:
Checkin' In

There was laughter in my life; my father saw to that. I fought sleep on Saturday nights, waiting for him to come home after a 12-hr day of standing on his feet to parch peanuts, play smut, tell jokes, and share his life stories. He would keep us laughing well into the night. There was good in my life; he saw to that as well. We lacked for nothing; in fact, we were certain to be the first to have those things my father determined to be necessities. From indoor plumbing to color television, we were the first on our block to progress with the times. School trips, materials, supplies, activities, very little happened without the Thomas girls in participation. Our summers were spent in Louisiana surrounded by the love of a great grandmother, grandmother, aunts, uncles, and cousins, filled with chinaberry wars, cool cups, and Ms. Monya's pears. But, let's face it, a brownie uniform was just not a necessity to my father; it was about the activities and the experiences, not the uniform. Besides, it was a running joke in the family that my father was cheap; he was not going to spend money on anything that was not a necessity. I clearly understand that he just didn't know that the Brownie uniform was a necessity to me, that my feelings of inadequacy were exacerbated when I was the only one without one [and I might not have been the only one]. I doubt he even knew that a select group of kids were being given violin lessons, and I was not in that group, but I wanted to be. How was a Black man from the back woods of Louisiana with no education, reared by a troubled mulatto father and a mother who spoke broken English, blessed with the G.I. Bill to learn a trade supposed to be able to psychoanalyze each of his four children? He was supposed to house, clothe, feed, protect, educate, and love them, teach them right from wrong, and that, he did. He did it for several years without the assistance of a wife. It was just me, the kid that I was. Nobody tells parents to "be careful; you just might have that one kid that is from neither Venus nor Mars, and every incident, great and small, that happens in her life is going to hit her hard and leave an indelible imprint." If there was a handbook entitled, "How to Tune In to the Individual Sensibility of Each One of Your Children", he would not have thought to read it anyway. He simply had no clue that I was just one of those kids. So, again, don't get me wrong; this is not a pity party.

This started out as an act of cleansing limiting beliefs, and, for the most part, still is. However, it is also about getting into my feelings, those that have lingered throughout my life, those that found their way into my psyche and took up residency during these formative years, wreaking havoc the rest of my life must be called out.

> I am discovering in this process that in addition to the experiences themselves, are <u>extenuating circumstances</u> that magnify them, i.e. age, personality, temperament, culture, even astrology, etc. ... VERY IMPORTANT

So, what I have discovered to this point, is that from the age of 5 to 11years, there were emotional experiences that left me feeling alone in the world, rejected, misunderstood, judged, betrayed, forgotten, unworthy, not good enough, not smart enough. Prior to age 5, I have few memories, and most of them have no emotional charge; they left me with no specific feelings, just questions maybe. This is not to say that every little detail of life must be summoned, regurgitated, dissected, and analyzed. It just happens that the experiences and words that do leave their mark, for many of us, are the negative ones.

[I read awhile back someplace that our brains are wired toward the negative for the sake of survival; we remember the negative and prepare for the negative as a means of protecting ourselves from lurking dangers. So, the negative experiences are the most impactful in our lives, for most of us anyway.]

What I have also discovered in this process, is that, in addition to being a survival mechanism, these "negative' experiences, which I prefer to call "emotionally charged" experiences, deposit feelings that grab our attention and won't go away because they are trying to tell us something, impart a message, guide us, direct us! Our job is to hear.

Obviously, between the ages of 5 and 11, I had not yet learned to hear. So, no, my life was not totally traumatic; I remember what I remember for a reason.

Following, is a tribute to the village that formed me, and further proof that I really was like every other kid, just different. <u>On Being Raised, but Not Like Corn</u> is a work of fiction, based on bits and pieces of true stories, featuring real people, woven together to acknowledge the beauty of growing up in the 60's and 70's, when there was a thing called the Black Community; it wasn't perfect, but it was there, and it was ours.

IN MEMORY
of
Ms. Evelyn
Mrs. Cloteal Dove
Ms. Clementine (Tine) Williams

On Being Raised, but Not Like Corn

Sharon threw a rock at Ethel. It hit Ms. Evelyn's mail box, the mail box, not Ms. Evelyn. But in a matter of seconds, Ms. Evelyn was at her gate, arms folded.

"Ethleeen! Who threw and hit my box?"

Ethel, always ready to turn state's evidence, quickly pointed to Sharon, coming up behind her, too tickled to be scared. Sharon turned, walking backwards, putting up a grand effort to shield her laughter from Ms. Evelyn, but I was bringing up the rear, and the more I crossed my eyes, wiggled my tongue, and stuck my finger up my nose, the harder Sharon's struggle to hide her laughter became. Her little round shoulders couldn't hold their posture any longer. They bounced up and down and threw her backward as she exploded with laughter just a few feet from Ms. Evelyn's gate. Sharon's sense of humor, a constant companion, had betrayed her once again.

"Oh! So, you think it's funny, hunh?"

Ms. Evelyn's fists were digging into her bony hips by now, and her eyes were squinting.

Sharon slowly rose to face Ms. Evelyn.

"Nohohoho ma'haham".

Coming up on the scene, trying to give an air that I was in no way involved in the rock throwing incident, I quickly found my composure, a feat at which I was adeptly skilled. Sharon tried several times to mock my stance, but each time a flood of air burst through her nostrils and she was laughing all over again.

"Yeah!" Squeaked Ms. Evelyn. "You think it's funny."

Ms. Evelyn's head bobbed with every word.

"You – think - it's - funny!"

For Sharon's sake, I really wished Ms. Evelyn's head wouldn't do that because it made her look like a cartoon character … Olive Oil! That's who she looked like, and she continued.

"Sposin' you'da dented my box, or knocked it down? You think it's funny to go tearin' up the neighborhood?"

We could have chorused the next sentence with her, but we dared not. "Thas why Black folks can't have nothin'!

Then came one we were not expecting.

"And sposin' you'da put out Ethleen's eye with that rock. Would it 'a' been funny?"

Dear God! Why did she have to say that? Surely, Sharon must have pictured Ethel with one eye, and probably with a patch over it because, I did. Sharon dropped to the ground, rolling with laughter. It was over. Ethel must have pictured the exact same thing, and though we knew what was next, we just couldn't help ourselves. We hit the dirt road.
Ms. Evelyn, with the quickness of at least 11 years practice we knew about, had grabbed a switch and was swatting our legs good. When the stings began to set in, and Ms. Evelyn had sufficiently gained our attention, we apologized.

"We sorry, Ms. Evelyn", we chorused.

We apologized for laughing, for throwing rocks...

"We sorry".

... for unpaved roads ...

"We sorry".

... for no street lights and no sidewalks ...

"We sorry".

For everything else Ms. Evelyn believed made conditions in the Black community a living hell, "a sin and a shame, just a sin and a shame", we apologized. We promised not to destroy the neighborhood, to make good grades, to go to college, come back and build up our people and our community, so help us God. But that, of course, as we knew, was not the end of it. In less the time it took us to walk half a block, Ms. Evelyn had called Mrs. Dove and relayed the whole incident.

We had barely cleared the magnolia tree which hung over the ditch and provided about ten steps worth of shade, and there stood Mrs. Dove, in the middle of her yard, hands on her hips. Mrs. Dove had one day off during the week from cleaning up some white lady's house, Friday. Whenever I walked past with Sharon and Ethel, which was rare, she usually waved real sweet and friendly like from her porch, sipping from a cup of mid-day coffee, but today, she was in her yard. We waved innocently, passing her gate.

"Heeey Mrs. Dove."

"Get back here." Mrs. Dove demanded, very unfriendly like. She wasn't shouting; she was frighteningly matter of fact.

"Yes ma'am", we sang in unison. Sharon was trying her best to be composed, but suddenly, just inside the gate, she ducked. So, I ducked and Ethel ducked, but not fast enough to miss the ripple of smacks right across the top of our heads, and they kept coming.

"Start actin' like you got some sense. You too smart to be clowns. On top of that, you're girls. Girls behave."

"What?!"

No, I didn't say it; I thought it. So, girls behave and boys get away with murder? Is that it?

"Yes ma'am", we refrained.

In the middle of our about face out of Mrs. Dove's yard, at the very next corner, catty corner from Mrs. Dove, we caught sight of Ethel's mama, opening the screen door. Sharon and I looked over at Ethel.

"Stop lookin' at Ethel! You all in this together!" We jumped, not expecting Mrs. Dove to still be barking behind us, our hearts already filling with dread.

Mrs. Robinson was coming down the front steps, wiping her hands on a cup towel. Mrs. Robinson always gave sermonettes on what the Lord expects of his children. If we could get through it without so much as a yawn or a snicker, Sharon and I were home free. But Mrs. Robinson had something else for us today. Not only did the Lord expect us to show the world how smart and intelligent Black children could be, today, on a bright and sunny Friday afternoon, the Lord expected us to know the 23rd Psalm, and he expected us to recite it, right then and there.

"The Lord is my Shepherd; I shall not want. He maketh me to lie down in green pastures ..."

Now, Sharon's family had known my family for years before moving away to California; in fact, it was her family's home address that I used at school. This was our 6th grade year, and they had just moved back to Houston. Sharon and I found each other in the first wave of integration zoning when we discovered we were giving the same address to go to school. Though we would lose each other again during the second wave of integration zoning, we had started to sync up. We had already discovered that our minds operated pretty much the same way.

I wondered; so, I knew Sharon wondered, and I wondered if Ethel wondered too, what the h-e-double toothpicks did green pastures have to do with rocks and mail boxes? So, just as we were rounding the valley of the shadow of death, I caught Sharon's eye, and it was, again, over. Before we knew it, we were rolling with laughter in the green pastures of Mrs. Robinson's front yard getting the cup towel whipping of our lives. As soon as Mrs. Robinson ran out of breath and felt certain that we were saved from hell and damnation, Sharon and I left Ethel to be led in the house by her right ear, and we sprinted all the way to the end of Morrow St.

Mr. Lott was a teacher; so, he hadn't come home yet and wouldn't have heard the news. Kelvin's parents worked 'til 5, and so did the Dorians. Past two vacant lots and Hailie

Wheeler's grandfather sittin' on his porch eatin' sugar cane, there was Miss Clementine, Sharon's mama; we called her Tine (pronounced Teen). She sat on the bottom step, a fly swatter in one hand, a bucket in the other. She fanned away flies with the fly swatter, all the while scooping up rocks and dropping them in the bucket. Right then, I wished I had stayed at Mable B. Wesley Elementary School and waited for my step-mother to pick me up, but it was Friday, and I had earned my Friday privilege of walking home from the school I was not supposed to be attending in the first place, with Sharon and Ethel. But no matter how I prayed, or how hard I looked, it would be awhile before my step mother's car rounded that bend, at the end of Morrow St. No matter how hard I feigned deafness, I could hear that bucket rattling up the driveway in our direction.

"So! You an' ya ace boon coon feel like throwin' rocks today, hunh Miss Anne? Do you? You feel like throwing rocks today, Miss Anne?"

"Miss Anne", those were the magic words, and she had already said them twice. Whoever Miss Anne was, she must have left a very bad impression on Black women, especially Tine. Whenever Tine called you Miss Anne, that meant she was not pleased. I looked at Sharon; Sharon looked at me. There was nothing funny.

PART II

The one you are looking for is you.

Osho

Not Gonna Call Me a Bull Dagger

I fell in love when I was 12, but it was an unrequited love, for a while anyway. It was unrequited because he didn't know. I was 12 and he was 17; enough said. He was tall and cute and had a nice fro, and he spoke to me. Every time he saw me, he spoke. That is all. So, there were two or three boyfriends until I won my love in a game of spin the bottle at the age of 14, but I didn't really like those in-the-meantime boys and they really didn't like me. M. C. Williams Jr., Sr. High School housed kids from 7th - 12th grade, all in one building. Some have called it an experiment, but I see it as a very bold move of self-determination by community leaders to ensure there was a community school for their children. So, as a 7th grader at M.C., there was the 10th grader who thought I was young, naïve, impressionable and wanted to be liked by the older boys and willing to give it up behind the Auto Mechanics building, but I was 12 and I wasn't about to give up anything. Then there was the 9th grade football player who I thought I might like, mainly because most of the Junior High cheerleaders had a boy on the football team they liked, but he decided I was a "hoe" because I kinda liked another boy in the Drama Club too, before I even met this football player, and somebody told him. Yeah, if a girl just "liked" more than one boy, she was a "hoe". So, after he yelled it out to all the cheerleaders and the football players on the bus, I didn't like him anymore. In fact, I was about to not like boys at all; then, we were forced to switch schools where I would meet a whole new crop of kids.

At the new school, I agreed to be "paired up" with a boy because he was my step- sister's boyfriend's brother and my other sister's boyfriend's friend, but mostly I figured it was the best way to escape being called a "bull dagger". That was a new word for me. It was an ugly, hateful word. The older kids laughed when they used it to describe a girl in our neighborhood. They were on the bus, saying it over and over again, laughing. I didn't want them saying that about me. I kinda liked that girl in our neighborhood, but she didn't like me; she liked my step-sister, let her tell it, who was known for stretching the truth, and probably instigated the whole bull dagger episode. Anyway, liking girls was unchartered territory. I had heard my eldest sister talk about one of our cousins who had a girlfriend; she seemed pretty indifferent about it. She was more upset that the "girlfriend" was forcing our cousin to leave a family function before it was over than she was about our girl cousin having a girlfriend. That was the extent of my knowledge. I just knew why they called her a bull dagger, and they were not gonna call me that.

I had enough problems fitting in already. I wasn't sweet and smiley, and didn't match my colors like my middle sister; I didn't dress fashionably and say crazy stuff to make people laugh like my step-sister; so, I wasn't popular like them. My middle sister and I had a book as kids called, Tag Along Tooloo. Well, I always felt like Tooloo. I wore glasses which fogged up when I got on the bus, to which my across the street neighbor thought it great to announce to everybody, pointing her pudgy, yellow finger at me. "Look at Norm's glasses! Look!" My clothes rarely fit because I always seemed to be in transition, in the middle of some kind of growth spurt. If it wasn't my breasts, it was my long legs, then my butt started to get wide, flat and wide. I was a mess, and I was supposed to make new friends at a new school?

So, I became that girl, the one who just wanted to fit in, who wanted to belong. For so many reasons, I just didn't. There was the one group of girls who laughed and talked with me in class, but not in the hallway; they met their real friends in the hallway. As soon as we hit the door heading out of the classroom, I was suddenly invisible. The other group actually said I was "stuck up", that I "high sided", as one girl put it. Dumb asses. Didn't they see me, looking like a raga-muffin? If they only knew how awkward I felt. I was a late bloomer in many ways, but managed to hide it. I didn't dress as well as they did, and I felt inferior, to well, everybody! Not even the heavy girl or the nerdy girl were interested in being my friend, and yes, there was one of each that I thought were great friend candidates.

The heavy girl was allowed to drive her mom's car to school, and she smoked. We fell into conversation one day and I asked if she would let me ride home with her. She did. We had a blast, me hanging out the window feeling the breeze, she puffing like a choo-choo train, but when I saw her after that, it was like the ride never happened. Then, I never saw her again. The nerdy girl read strange books. So, I asked if she wanted to trade books. When I was done, I'd give her the book I was reading, and she'd give me the book she had just read. I was an avid reader, but I was not reading a novel at the time; I was actually never into novels, but it was an ice breaker. I found a novel to exchange, and we did. <u>Tango in Paris</u>, I had no idea what the book was about. I never got to read it. My step-sister told my step-mother I was reading an X-rated book; so, my step-mother threw it away; she wouldn't even let me return it to its owner. So much for that friend.

I sat on the picnic table in the yard one day, and wondered:

Do I stink? I don't like baths; they take up too much time, but I do bathe. Is it because my clothes are never quite right? I actually have a good eye for fashion; I could be a fashion model. I just don't have the right clothes. Daddy never gives me enough money to buy anything that suits my tastes. Deirdre guilts her mom into giving her more money over what Daddy gives us all, and she typically buys everything I like, but can't afford. Joby is a saver and always has extra cash; besides, I think Kathy and Pam slip her a few dollars here and there for babysitting Sheky and Chris. So, I with the few dollars squeezed out of my father, buy what I can. I'm 13 and I've done this since I was 11.

[Something I've always wondered and pisses me off every time I think about it. Who sends an eleven year old into Joske's to do school shopping alone? I came out with 5 dresses, same style, with variations of the same three colors, all technically too small. An adult female would have been able to see that the way the dresses rode up on my butt, they would be too small in about two months. Well, there was no adult female in my life who cared what I looked like; so, such was the case, and from age 11, my wardrobe never seemed to catch up.]

Not to mention I'm a tomboy, a nicer term than bull dagger, and my clothes always end up torn or stained. Everything I borrow from Joby ends up torn or stained. So, if I don't stink, if it's not my clothes, what is it? Does everybody know? Can they look at me and tell that I'm a bull dagger? Is there something that gives it away? I don't know how bull daggers act, but whatever I'm doing has to change so nobody knows. They're not gonna call me a bull dagger.

I decided, sitting out there on the picnic table that day, that being smart was definitely out. I had learned that in Elementary School, and if only to remind me of the fact, in Middle School, I had already been sent to the office for telling my English teacher how to spell the word "chitterlings"; she had misspelled it. This little white woman, with a Russian surname, actually thought the spelling was "c-h-i-t-l-i-n-s". "Honey, I read the bucket every New Year's Eve"; I told her. Then, I looked it up and showed it to her in the dictionary. She said I was being insubordinate and sent me to the office. Then, I was browbeaten and ridiculed by my History teacher for rolling my eyes when she said that slavery was the best thing to happen to the starving people of Africa. The Preacher's Kid, the only other Black kid in the classroom, and I, mentally checked out of the class and retaliated in the only childish way we knew, by making private jokes about her floods (pants worn well above the ankle that were meant to stop well below the ankle).

It was the year of White is Right, about 1972-1973; I don't know when the Preacher's Kid got the memo, but I had learned in 6th grade that my father expected my step-mother to handle all things education, and she was not going to stand up for me against anybody or anything at Eisenhower Jr./Sr. High School; white is right. The first and only time, ever, a teacher had called my parents, she didn't bother to inquire as to what could have been going on in my life. The P.E. teacher had phoned to say that I was unsociable with the other girls in class. Was it that I didn't dress out? No. Was it that I didn't participate in class or follow directions? No. Had I been rude or disrespectful? Unh unh. I was reprimanded for not being sociable in class. I don't know how the teacher actually broached the issue; she might have been genuinely concerned that a girl such as I had difficulty fitting in, and possibly wanted to alert my step-mother in the event she was raising a psychopath who might one day kill her in her sleep. Still, no questions were asked. "Do the other girls not like you? Do you feel out of place? Do you have the lowest self-esteem in the history of mankind?" Nothing. So, the Preacher's Kid and I took matters into our own hands, and when the History teacher walked into the classroom, we would lift our legs to avoid the flood-waters she brought in with her. It was our joke; it was all we had to fight with. Before class one day, while the teacher was still standing by her door for class change, the Preacher's Kid wrote on the blackboard, "Whoosh!" It took her half the class period to notice it. When she did, she looked straight at him and threatened to send him to the office. I can't remember if she did or not. So, no, being smart was over-rated in my opinion, totally not worth the headaches.

I sought out the stage. I had been in Speech and Drama during 7th grade and it had been my life. Though the Speech and Drama program at this school could in no way measure up to my former school, I needed the stage. There, I was very adept at being someone other than me. I was the Old Woman in "Pullman Car Hiawatha" and won Best Actress in competition for it. I was Salome' in "Sunday Costs Five Pesos", the only 8th grader allowed to participate in the High School UIL One Act Play. This school was Jr. and Sr. High together also; so, that's how the Drama teacher got around it. Unfortunately, I ended up dropping out of the show because my step-sister skipped school, and in the search for her, the Administrators found out we had moved out of the district. Never mind that my dad still owned and paid taxes on the house in the district, and on several other properties; we were ousted. Before the oust, I had tried out for emcee of the Talent Show; I really wanted to sing with Soul Patrol, a group that my step-sister and her friends started, but I was quickly excluded from that venture; so, I went to the emcee audition. Everybody in the auditorium knew I was the best; they had to select me! But they didn't have to let me actually emcee … aahh white people! I even got a new outfit for it, something I liked. I gave a rousing welcome to the audience, but every time I tried to step forward and introduce the next act, I was gently pushed aside. A cute little white girl, one of the cheerleaders, dressed like a Raggedy Anne doll, would bounce onto stage holding a very nicely painted sign bearing the name of the next act. Wow, they had gone all out to keep my Black ass off the stage. I guess if I'd been singing and dancing, it would've been okay. So, I spent the entire Talent Show, probably one of the most talented kids in the room, in my new outfit, offstage. Thus, the stage was a bust, and showing how smart I could be was out of the question. So, where does a 13 year old who doesn't fit in, fit in? In her head, nowhere; it's not gonna happen, especially if she's riding home on the bus and somebody blurts out, "Norm is a bull dagger!" I couldn't let that happen. But how?

The Slow Drag Girl

I wanted to swing out. There was a cool new swing out dance in the early 70's that involved the guy pulling the girl in to sit on his knee then swinging her back out, with a few other twirly moves, but nobody would teach it to me. I was a pretty good dancer; so, I knew I could learn it. I watched closely and was picking it up, but I never got the chance to actually do it. The guys who came to the house to see my sisters didn't want to dance with me; they wanted to dance with my sisters. There was one guy who would tolerate me for about 5 minutes while he pretended not to care that my step-sister, who knew he was there, refused to come out of her room. The guy they paired me with couldn't even dance; he was very nice, but he just wanted to sit close and rest his arm on my neck. That was so uncomfortable; so, whenever I saw him coming up the walk, I suddenly got the cramps. I was such a good actress, my Dad believed me and, thinking something warm would help, made coffee, which I finally had to explain would only make the cramps worse because of the caffeine. How I knew that, I have no idea, but I was not about to drink hot coffee. I thought this one other boy would teach me, but I didn't realize until his mother came home and ordered me out of her house that the swing out was not his intention. It was when she looked at me from head to toe as if she possessed x-ray vision and had spied something vile inside of me, that I realized what she thought. I felt so small, so judged, so misunderstood.

So, when the fast records came on at the Homecoming Dance, nobody asked me to dance, but on the slow jams, the boys knocked themselves over trying to get to me, because I was that girl. It only took one dance, with one boy, and I was The Slow Drag Girl. The Slow Drag Girl let the boys cop a feel. She let them dance too close. She let them hold too tight. She let them drag too slow. I basically let them screw me standing up, all to be included, part of the group, but I still wasn't.

All the Black kids had gravitated to one side of the Cafeteria and the white kids to the other. A group of 8th grade girls that I really wanted to be friends with was there. I went to where they were standing. The pretty one with the really long hair who was nice to me in class, but ignored me in the hallway, who I thought I could really be friends with was great with the swing out. She said her older brothers taught her. On the swing out songs, somebody always grabbed her hand. When she was done dancing, she went back to her friends; she even had a few white friends who came to the Black side just to hang out with her. I wanted to laugh when they laughed, but I couldn't find my way in. What if I did, and they looked at me all crazy like? So, I stood there for a while, watching. It all looked like so much fun. I don't remember why my sisters chose not to go to the dance, but they weren't there; so, I was pretty much alone. Finally, somebody asked me to dance … slow.

He pulled me close, so I went. I knew what a hard on was, and I felt it coming. I just didn't care. I gave him the ride he was looking for. Surely, the others were watching, and he went back to report. I must have screwed every Black boy in the Cafeteria. Here's the worse part, those boys, all friends of my sisters, who let me ride with them to the dance, and noticed me long enough to dry hump me on the dance floor, did not even offer me a ride home. We all lived within three or four blocks of each other. I came to the conclusion that I had to be some kind of apparition that went in and out of sight. "Now you see me; now you don't." At the un-cool age of 13, I got it. Those guys didn't see me. They could've been screwing a phantom for all they cared; they were boys. And they surely couldn't give me a ride home. They would have to acknowledge that I was real and they had just gotten off screwing their friends' little sister. Yeah, it occurred to me that night that I was fucking invisible; for everybody's sanity, I had to be.

[Hell, you have to be invisible, when you're in the middle of a snow-ball fight and nobody throws any snowballs at you. My Dad and my older sister, looking out of the living room window, they saw it. It didn't snow often in Houston, but this was a doozy. It actually stuck and was thick enough for snow angels, snowmen, and snowball fights. So, I went out to join the fun, but I had forgotten; shit, I was invisible. "They're not paying attention to you, Norm!" My sister yelled and my Dad echoed. "Come on back and let 'em play". Let THEM play. Hell, it was my yard! Why they had come down to my yard, I'm not sure. My sisters were not out there; maybe they hoped they would be. A male cousin, who had come to live with us for a minute, was out there, and me. So, I came in and watched other kids enjoy a snow-ball fight in my yard, and was supposed to be okay with it. Well, that's what happens when you're invisible. If they had thrown one snowball in my direction, it would have required that they acknowledge my presence as something other than The Slow Drag Girl. They couldn't do that; I guessed.]

Upgrade: From Invisibility to a She-Dog in Heat

My step-mother bestowed the distinction upon me when I came into the house one evening after hanging out in the drive. She said, "Nahrm, you're like a she-dog in heat." It took me a minute to digest the initial shock of the words, then process their meaning. Literal child, grammatical genius with serious syntaxical prowess that I was, I mentally diagrammed the sentence and though I immediately substituted the word "bitch" for "she-dog", and "horny" for "heat", having those words point back to the pronoun, "you", followed by the verb of *being*, "are" stumped me for a minute. It was the 70's; neither George Clinton nor the Funkadelics had ever referred to sisters as bitches; so, it was not common and totally not cool to call a sister a bitch in those days. Even if she possessed some psychic power, some hoe-dar with which she detected the presence of a hoe, or if maybe a little birdie had told her about the Homecoming Dance, then her mother-wit should have kicked in and informed my step-mother that I wasn't the horny one at the dance, just the screwing post. Thus, after that eternal minute, I concluded that she possessed nothing, neither psychic power, hoe-dar, a little birdie, mother-wit, nor tact. I hovered a few of those seconds over the word, "like"; yeah, she did say, "like" a she-dog in heat, but I was 13. Similes were the devices of cowards.

Here's the thing. Our house sat right at the top of the neighborhood, so to speak, where the two main arteries met, perpendicular to one another; ours was the cross street. Can you picture that? I'm not good at imagery. My sisters would often sit on the trunk of the car, at the edge of the drive; so, their friends and other school kids would stop and chat. Sometimes, there would be a whole gathering, everybody laughing and joking around, having a good time. I didn't join in too often because I always ended up the brunt of my step-sister's jokes. She and one of our across the street neighbors were always mocking somebody, and many times, that somebody was me. So, when they weren't around, I started sitting out myself, just before dusk. It wasn't about boys. There was just something about a group of kids hanging out that I wanted to experience. We didn't worry about fights or drive-by's in those days. When the boys did stop, they were only asking where my sisters were, what they were doing, when they were coming back. It had nothing to do with me.

What my step-mother obviously did not know, I was The Slow Drag Girl, a ghost just trying to max out the time that I might be visible to the naked eye, knowing full well, it will take another School Dance for anybody to notice me again. So, while her words stung and stung deep, mainly because they sounded so nasty coming out of her mouth, little did my step-mother know, for a slow drag girl who apparently moved in and out of visibility to the outside world, being a horny bitch was an upgrade.

Didn't I Almost Have it All?
Checkin' In

I was fairly intelligent, made good grades until I realized grades didn't change anything; so, the grades just fell in my lap. I spoke very well, was "articulate" as is said about Black people whose tongues are not so thick as to impede their speech. I was talented; I could write, act, dance, and hold a tune. I wasn't the prettiest flower in the vase, but I wasn't all that bad looking under my glasses; in fact, my hazel eyes, considered an anomaly were always quite striking. I even have a pretty decent head of hair. I should have been the envy of every teen girl I met. I almost had it all. I just didn't know it. I couldn't see the forest for the trees. I was the forest. I just wanted to be one of the trees.

In retrospect, I have wondered if others simply perceived that I knew I almost had it all, and responded to me as such, from their perception. I have wondered if I set people off, tried too hard, required too much energy for coexistence with others. I am not one to blame others for what I think, feel, or experience. I am not afraid to look inside myself; so, these, and others, are retrospective musings. At the time, I just knew what I felt, and in my early years of experiences, I journeyed through feeling alone in the world, forgotten, unworthy, not good enough, not smart enough, alienated, outcast, and damn near invisible on a good day, to feelings of being too big for the space I was in, having worn out my welcome. It's what I felt. Now, I'm asking. What did these feelings come to say? When you're 14 and you feel forgotten, you ask. "How can I be remembered?" When you feel rejected, you ask, "What can I do to be accepted?" You ask. "How do I turn this around so I can feel that I am enough, worthy, welcomed, that I belong and I am free to be me?" You keep asking the same questions, not realizing they are the wrong questions. So, the answers you get, do you no good. When you don't know that you almost have it all, even though that still voice that you started arguing with when you were six keeps trying to tell you otherwise, you keep trying to get what you think you are missing.

Actually, your ass is insane, because the definition of insanity is "doing the same thing, expecting something different." When you're 14 and don't know any better, that's what you do. When you're a forest in your own right, trying to be a tree simply doesn't work for you, but you don't know that's the problem. So, I was 14, and insane.

Too bad I didn't see the world like Groucho Marx who once said, "I don't want to belong to any club that will accept me as a member." But I didn't. I wanted to be a member.

I almost had it all, and didn't know it; so, Brandy was right, "almost ain't good enough".

Me, almost.

Looking for God in All the Wrong Places

When no one sees you, you begin to wonder if you exist. On those rare occasions when you are seen, but what the observers see and what you know they should be seeing are incongruent, you graduate to the big question. Who am I and why am I here? The search for that answer, for most of us, is first asked in our places of worship, where God, the source of all things and all of us is supposed to live. Hell, if the answer isn't there; there is no answer. That's what you think.

By my early teens, I had grown to love church. No one had to make me go. The church we attended was relatively new and the youth program was just getting developed, but suddenly I found myself belonging someplace with people who accepted me. I was reconnecting with people I'd known my whole life, with kids I actually shared common interests with, common family ties, and community history, like Lynda, my one, constant friend in Elementary School [until I was zoned, then re-zoned, and the preacher's kid was zoned in the process; so, she kicked my ass to the curb], and Sharon. Remember Sharon, who threw the rock? It's the 70's; we're loving life. We're doing all the stupid stuff kids do and we're surviving; we're having a blast. We take youth trips. We've got the best matrons in the world, a group of open-minded women who encourage us to think and question. One says she can actually see God in me! "Norma Thomas knows the Lord!" She said one day. I was as shocked as everybody else in the room, but truthfully, I was probably seeking God's face just a little bit harder than the rest.

> *People who fit don't seek.*
> *The seekers are those that don't fit.*
> Shannon L. Alder

Perhaps, I just needed to ask God some questions that none of the rest needed answers to. So, I was beginning to think; maybe, I'm not invisible after all.

Lynda, Sharon, and I, at some church function; I'm sure.

But if this isn't the story of my life! I'm suddenly transported back in time, six or seven years ago, to fourth grade, when, as soon as I had found my trump card, the game changed. In creeped that sense, that feeling of having out-stayed my welcome. Older Black people used to say, "Don't wear your welcome out." Suddenly, I felt as if I had. Even now, it sounds weird and unrealistic; it doesn't make sense. It didn't make sense then; so, I denied my feelings; I brushed them off. Heck, I was the resident skit writer; I sang in the choir, ushered on the Youth Usher Board, read the Church Announcements, played piano in Sunday School. Yet, it persisted, that sense of being judged and misunderstood, of living under a microscope on borrowed time in a borrowed space. I wondered what I had done. Did I try too hard and come off phony? Was I overbearing? Once before, I had felt that there was not enough space in the world for me. I felt it again, like the world, my world was too small. Yet, I laughed through the pain of it all. I was 14, and my friend, Sharon, was nuts; hell, we were all nuts; all we did was laugh at one thing or another. Laughing and joking, but on pins and needles most of the time, waiting for the moment my world would spin me off into another space and time, or to a place where neither existed.

Back in the day, we had Night Service. The day began with Sunday School, about 9am. From there we went straight into Worship Service, about 11am, then a break for Sunday Dinner about 2:00pm, with just enough time to get back to church or go fellowship with another church about 3 or 3:30pm. Some church, if not our own, was always having Church Anniversary, Pastor's Anniversary, Women's Day, Men's Day, Usher's Annual Day, Mission Sunday, 100 Youth in White, 100 Women in Hats, 100 Men in Suits;

there was always something. We ended our day of worship at Night Service, about 7:30pm. However, a few years before back in the day, there would first be BYPU and Youth Meeting at 6:30.

One particular Sunday night, we were in Nigh Service; nothing had happened out of the ordinary. The choir sang. The preacher preached. Those of us kids who were there did our usual; we talked a little, giggled a little, listened a little, and passed snacks down the row. A feeling suddenly came over me. I can't describe it to this day. Everyone started asking what was wrong. I couldn't say because I didn't know. Maybe something the preacher said struck a nerve; I don't know, but I grew quiet, sullen. Church was over and I stood outside the store-front building, tears streaming down my face. My daddy came out and I asked him, "What happened to my Mama"? To be honest, I'm not sure if that was the right question. I think I spoke the first words that would come out of my mouth. I think I really wanted to ask him, "What is wrong with me?"

My dad was and still is a very simple man, meat and potatoes, it is what it is kinda guy who lets everything just roll off his back, stays in the middle of the road. If we wished for rain, he would admonish us that construction workers lose work when it rains. If we sang, "rain, rain go away; come again another day", he would remind us that farmers needed rain to grow crops. If my nephews yelled at the football player on television, "Hit him!" My father would ask, "Why would you want them to hit the man?

Don't you know that man has a family to take care of?" That's who he was; he's changed a bit in his old age; but, he still doesn't seem to care one way or the other. My dad, that night, had no answer for me. Each time my mind has traveled back to that incident, I've gotten the feeling [there's that word again – feeling] that he felt the real question, the sponsoring question, and truly had no answer.

"We'll talk about it when we get home".

In the car, my step-mother quelled whatever attempt he would have made to answer with her dismissive air.

"What's wrong with her?"

"Just thinkin' 'bout the past"; he answered.

So, we rode home from church with her going on about something nobody really wanted to hear. My daddy and I didn't discuss it when we got home. He asked if I was okay and I said I was. I was not, but that's how we did things. Besides, what could he do? Perhaps, the burden of visibility and the microscope of scrutiny had become too great for one accustomed to not being seen at all, therefore not addressed, included, or engaged. Where there was once only sporadic attention before, or I was idiotic enough to step into the spotlight, now there was what felt like an examination of my every move, every word, and subsequent misjudgment or total misunderstanding of it all. When one person's jokes and shenanigans are classified as silly and mischievous, but yours as borderline vindictive, isn't that cause to wonder what is wrong with you? When your church friend's mom tells you she didn't give you an invitation to a special event, but gave one to the other friend because that friend is "special", does that not make you want to smell your armpits, so to speak? When you pour your heart into a speech, search the bible for scriptural support the way you were taught and give the speech of your life and an adult tells you "your speech was musky", but your friend's speech, which you also wrote, was "simply wonderful", is that not cause for ponder? Yet, I AM the common denominator in my life. So, here I am God, at your house, asking all the questions I can think to ask. I thought I had graduated to "Who am I and why am I here?" Yet, I find myself back at square one. "What's wrong with me?"

Well, God didn't speak. Either I hadeth no ear to hear, or the church just wasn't where God was. One of the deacons said, not to me directly, "You have to go into your secret closet and pray." I was a literal child; so, I did. God wasn't there either.

Middle Finger to the Line

I'm sure it's obvious by now that I would become one of those teens who acted out their frustrations with life. I crossed the line on many occasions. I stopped caring what people thought. Forced to change Middle Schools well after the middle of the year, I had pretty much given up on fitting in. I had become the classic "dark teen". Being smart, friending whoever showed up, slow dragging my soul into a dark pit, even speech and drama was the stuff of people who cared. I didn't. I was still pretty active in church though, but because we were all getting older and school activities were taking us in different directions, we were less in the spotlight, and my friends and I began to spend less time together. I was developing as a public speaker, and had ceased to look to the church elders for approval. I was finding God on my own terms. The rest of it, just didn't matter anymore.

At school, I was absent. I skipped. I slept. My step-mother dropped me off at school, and I waited for the tail of her Grandville to round the corner to the school where she then taught, and I disappeared in the other direction. One of my church buddies attended the same school; he was Clyde to my Bonnie. We skipped as far away as we could, on foot. One day we got the idea to hit a Seven-Eleven. I found something to purchase with my lunch money, which my daddy was still doling out in quarters and dimes. While at the counter waiting for my partner in crime, I engaged the clerk in "erudite banter". Impressed with my knowledge of nonsense and the ability to express it clearly, he never asked why I wasn't in school. Meanwhile, the remainder of our fare was being tucked down into the socks of my accomplice. We paid for a few items, and made off with the rest. That day, we walked to a totally different school district, eating snacks and chatting, about what, I have no remembrance.

When I did remain in school, I slept, allowing the little white boys who shared my table in Science to complete my work. I spent P.E. in the restroom. I was horrible at volleyball. Besides, I had appeared in P.E. class wearing my sister's High School sweater because my step-mother refused to purchase the required sweatshirt, insisting it was too late in the year and did not matter, but it was P.E. We were required to dress out. The sweatshirt was required. It mattered. I never understood her logic. So, after several days of not dressing out and getting a grade cut, I grabbed my sister's pull over sweater from High School which was at the top of my closet with a few of her old maternity clothes, which I had also begun to wear. I tried to turn it inside out so no one would see the MCW. Or was it a big H? Whatever it was, they saw it, and some of the girls laughed, girls from my new neighborhood. So, P.E. was out. Success at disappearing, in Middle School, was nothing less than rehearsal for encore performance in High School.

I was back in school with my sisters; it was High School; so, I was willing to give it a shot. I returned to Speech and Drama, went to a few contests, even starred in a play, which members of my church came to see. I joined the Band and the Dance Squad, until football season was over and I could get my schedule changed. I'm guessing it was just too late. I had embraced my darkness and there seemed no turning back. By this time, also, it didn't take much to set me off in the opposite direction of the rest of the world. An English teacher commented in my poetry journal that I had a lot of anger in me. I later learned they said that of all Black girls who displayed non-compliant behavior. The very same girl who had bullied me in Kindergarten was in this class, and was always trying to get me to put my desk in a group circle. Really? You think I'm going to sit in a circle with you? Flashback, Bully Girl! Besides, who writes in a fucking circle? Three years before, I would have jumped at the opportunity, but honey that ship had sailed.

So, I disappeared at lunch time to screw in the park, with my clothes on, of course. I cared a little bit about not getting pregnant. Most days I made it back to campus for the last class of the day. I liked Mrs. Jones. I was always late, but I showed up. She knew my stuck locker story was a lie and getting old, but she let me in anyway. It was in her class that I learned that Africa was considered the "Dark Continent". She explained why and it was the most interesting thing I had heard all year; it was probably the only thing I learned that year. Somehow, I managed to pass all of my classes with only a "C" in Math. Who could pass that class? There was no teaching going on, just white kids doing what the hell they wanted. It was the same way in Drama. The teacher had no control; he smoked like a train; his room was a filthy mess; one girl and her boyfriend actually spent the entire class screwing under the old curtains which were piled up on the classroom stage. One boy I thought I liked, who lived in our neighborhood (more and more Blacks were moving in) was so stuck on himself and obviously thought I was so desperate that he told me I would have to walk him to class and carry his books before he would consider "going with me". I took those books, dropped them to the floor, and walked away. I slept through Science, snacked through Spanish with Joby (I was good in Spanish), and spent a lot of time in detention because she was driving that year and made me late for school every day.

Did I mention earlier that I had begun to cross the lines? The lines between caring and not caring, respect and disrespect were not only blurring with every year, by the time I was 16, it was middle finger to the line. I had no fucks to give and nobody noticed.

[I am just now realizing how into the negative numbers those fucks actually were that I had to give. I crossed a lot of lines during that time. It was the 70's; the lines were not as blurred as they are today. Were I a different person, those days I got up the courage to or had sunken to such depths that I threw up the middle finger to the lines and to life, might have been moments of empowerment.

Amazingly, nobody was running to be our mentors in the 70's, or somebody probably would have recognized it for what it was. To the contrary, we had just come out of the Civil Rights Movement, and as a people, we were moving on up, showing the world that we could integrate and assimilate. Nobody had time to be wrestling with teenage issues. You fell your ass in line; that's what you did, down South anyway. Black folks had been through too much for you to be showing your ass. That's what Black folks would say. Still, I had some days when my fucks to give were as invisible as I had been.]

Crossing the line, what line? Middle finger to the line.

And They Called it Puppy Love: I

So, how did a girl of 14 attract the attention of a boy turning 19 years old? Was it how I read from the dictionary every time he visited his grandmother down the street and just happened to drop by, and just happened to find me reading the dictionary? Every house had a set of World Book, Britannica, Compton's, or Funk & Wagnall's Encyclopedia. When our two households merged, ours and my step-mother's, we ended up with all of them. I read through them often, especially the little skinny ones that were topic specific. I was a reader. I soaked up information. I was curious about the world, the universe. My sisters thought it cute to call me Miss Funk & Wagnall whenever I saw something or heard something I had read about and was excited and crazy enough to try and share it, and whenever I corrected their grammar, which was all the time. Upon discovering that I had a crush on an older boy, my thought went to how much smarter than I he had to have been; so, I set about learning new words by reading the World Book Dictionary. On those occasions I saw him walking up the street from his grandmother's house, I would grab the dictionary and impress him with my desire to expand my mind. He actually took note of it one day and asked, "Are you reading the dictionary?" When I responded, "Yeah, I read it all the time. I like learning new words", he didn't even laugh, not even a smirk. He didn't look at me strangely. He just said, "Oh". If not my affinity for the dictionary, then maybe it was the detail with which I explained the many uses of the screwdriver set my parents had bought from him when he was in Junior Achievement? I used it to tighten the drawers and cabinets in the kitchen; there was one small enough to tighten the screws on my eyeglasses. I showed him. He listened. Nope, I didn't give it up, and he didn't ask for it. It's important to know that this almost 19year old was every bit of 14 himself. For me, that has sufficed as explanation enough.

We were friends. We laughed a lot, clowned around a lot, kissed, and eventually, screwed, with our clothes on, a lot. We held the phone late into the night saying nothing, listening to each other breathe, a lot. We did crazy teenage stuff with our friends from church. He accepted me. He was my friend; he had an afro; I thought he was cute. That was enough. The mother of this almost 19year old wasn't too fond of me, I guessed. I think she thought I was giving it up looong before I was. In fact, it was rumored around church that I was pregnant long before I even lost my virginity. I let everybody think it for a few Sundays. Whenever I'd get up to make the Church Announcements, I'd rub my stomach like I had seen pregnant women do. I think my daddy had heard the rumors and also believed I had lost my virginity.

On one of the rare occasions that I remained at school, I

was in class with the cramps and asked if I could go to the clinic. Utilizing my natural acting ability, I made the cramps far worse than they were and asked if I could call my daddy to pick me up.

[I must add that this feat would, on a few occasions, come back to bite me. Times I was being most vulnerable, open, and honest, I was accused of merely acting. That's a painful accusation; but, it is what it is.]

So, my daddy picked me up and I asked him to stop at the store for pads. This man, who would tunnel through mountains for his girls, usually came out of the store, to our horror, with pads in his hands, for the world to see, no bag! Today, he came out with tampons. I told him I didn't wear tampons, which I didn't because they hurt. He insisted that I did. I said I didn't. He said I did. We went back and forth that way for a few minutes until he said he needed to get back to his barbershop. I think that was his way of trying to find out if I was still a virgin. You know that's what folks thought; girls who wore tampons were no longer virgins. So, I was stuck with tampons and boy do I have a tampon story, but this is not the place for it.

So, this almost 19year old's mother made very off-color remarks to me and about me on numerous occasions; I never told him. I never mentioned it to anybody. I was accustomed to being judged by people with no knowledge of what was going on inside of me. Hell, I had been bullied, thrown into a retarded class, lied on, rejected, and discriminated against before leaving grade school, not to mention I lived with a woman who was a pro a belittling me on a daily basis. I had been The Slow Drag Girl and a she-dog in heat, had escaped being called a bull dagger, and was still practically invisible. So, by then, I had not only learned to store my pain and mask it; I was 14, and though it was a total lie, told myself I had no fucks to give and behaved as such. Remember? Middle finger to the fucking line! She hurt my feelings and made me feel very small, but I had to tell myself I didn't care. Her son was my first love and the love of my life and that was that.

Truth is, if he didn't strike up a conversation, I had nothing to talk about, and though on most occasions, if I did have something to say, and the words remained stuck in my throat, I never felt compelled or forced to say anything. He was good at conversation. He made me laugh. He treated me like I belonged in the room. He took up for me. With him, I was home, or at least I thought I was. To him, I could escape from harsh words and crossed eyes. I can remember so often in his presence just wanting to scream, but simply having somebody understand the source of my agony was enough. I later realized that's why I kissed so long and passionately. Kissing was the volcanic eruption of all my inner feelings; kissing was the maximum emotional expression my outward self could afford. So, that's why we kissed a lot. That's why my sun rose and set in him.

Williams High Forensic is Groovy

"Williams High Forensic is groovy, all you have to do is try it. If you feel that you cannot make it then you better get down to true grit. Those of us who've already made it, we feel that you can make it too. So come on and nah - nah - nah - naah - nah, or your dreams never will come true. Hey, hey, hey!"

M. C. Williams Jr. High School Speech and Drama Club 1971-1972. The faces are masked to protect the innocent and avoid law suits, except for my friend Sharon on the end. She promised not to sue.

The "nah - nah - nah - naaah – nah" indicates words I have forgotten or never knew. I was in 7th grade at M. C. Williams Jr.-Sr. High School when I first heard the upper classmen of the Drama Club, Die Gruppe, sing this little ditty. I wanted to be in Die Gruppe. As a 7th grader, I was in Speech and Drama, but it wasn't Die Gruppe; you became a part of Die Gruppe at the High School level, 9th grade, after earning so many points for performances and competitions. Unfortunately, before that would happen I'd be snatched away to another school, then another. After three schools and three Speech and Drama clubs that would not compare to Die Gruppe in any way, slow-dragging, shop-lifting, school-skipping my way down the path to hell and destruction, there would come a soft tap on my shoulder, inviting me back. Though I was no longer a student at M.C., my 10th and 11th grade summers had been spent there in Summer Theatre Workshop.

Performing in an African dance pre-show for *To Be Young, Gifted & Black*. Every night the name of our tribe changed. We were the first African American theatre group to perform on Miller Outdoor Theatre stage.

Summer 1976, I was going into my senior year at Waltrip HS; God already knew it was not going to be pretty. So, as the Summer Theatre Workshop drew to a close, Mr. C. Lee Turner urged me to enroll in the Magnet School of Communications that was coming to MC that next year. It wasn't a Theatre Magnet School, for political reasons we guessed, but it would do. It was my senior year of high school; rarely does a student want to switch schools at senior year. It was do or die for me; I had sense enough to know that.

*Thanks Mr. Turner so very much for that literal tap on the shoulder, summer, 1976, inviting me to return home to my MCW roots. It changed the course of my life. We've had our ups, downs, ins and outs, but I remain eternally grateful to you my teacher, my mentor, my colleague, my friend. At the writing of this memoir, we are preparing to re-name
the M. C. Williams Auditorium
to The C. Lee Turner Performing Arts Center.*

1977, performing a duet scene from *Don't Bother Me I Can't Cope* for Francis Foster and the cast of "Sty of the Blind Pig." They were performing at the Alley Theatre, a rarity for Black actors in those days. We saw the show, had lunch with them, then did an evening of performances and Q&A.

I broke character that night, while performing a scene from *The Amen Corner,* in the role of Sis. Odessa. I thought it was something my character would laugh at so I tried to play it off, but everybody insisted I just broke character.

Francis Foster redeemed me later that night saying she and the *Sty* actors broke character every night at the window scene. They just couldn't help laughing.

So, I'm a senior in high school with finally a reason to get up every morning, to actually go to school and stay there, to pass my classes, and even fight for my grades; you'd think I'd be the happiest child on earth. I was, for a minute.

[You should know the pattern by now. Every time I found a new angle of existence, something to plant me and give me roots, something that said I belonged somewhere and dealt me a trump card to get ahead of the game or at least stay in the game, the game changed.]

I had learned back in first grade to ignore that still, soft voice in my head or heart, or where ever it was, that obviously knew nothing about me or about life in general, because it never seemed to see what I saw right in front of me, my reality. It had been my constant companion; yet, I didn't respect it much, didn't believe what it had to say because, hell, it always had some lame-brained excuse for everything or was trying to tell me I didn't see what I just saw. I could neither bank nor count on it. We engaged in many debates and impassioned arguments. It had, on occasion been sort of warm and comforting, but I couldn't depend on it. So, I paid it no never mind when it said that I belonged back at MCW, that I was okay, that I had the same amount of talent as everybody else, that I could take that talent, my really good SAT score, and all that scholarship money to the university of my choice. Then, right on cue, there came another voice; some loud mouth that moved in and took up residence and started out talking everybody. Sometimes, I would sit and listen to the two of them. The soft one that had been with me the longest never spoke above a whisper, and that actually pissed me off. It was always after the fact that I realized the still soft voice had spoken. "Speak up!" I yelled. It didn't. Oh, but the loud mouth. Jesus!

[Later in life I learned the names usually given to each of these voices, Spirit and Ego. Even later did I realize, there were three! The whisperer, the loud mouth, and me. Yeah, I actually had a voice of my own.]

This wasn't a feeling. I was accustomed to feeling some sort of way about my experiences, but this was different. This was direct communication. Everything I had felt up to this point was a result of something that had taken place outside myself, a result of experiences, emotional residue, like a virus, settling in my bones and in my organs, eating away at the fiber of my being. This was different. Though I was sure I had heard it before; now, it just seemed louder, much louder.

[Why now?]

"You do know you haven't been in theatre as long as everybody else, don't you?"

"Summer workshop was fun and games girl this is business and you ain't ready."

"See? You can't sing. She went and told everybody you

were just hollering."

"MaFaye already asked you 'Who do you think you are? What makes you think you can be like Ruby Dee, Cicely Tyson, and Diahann Carroll?' Well?"

"Girl don't pay attention to Sis. Thornton. She just calls you little Cicely to be nice."

"They weren't really clapping for you at the Talent Show; they were clapping for the dancers behind you."

"Why are you so immature? Everybody is way ahead of you. Grow up!"

So now the game had a new player, or a regular player suddenly feeling she had to vie for her position. If I had ever in my life felt unsure of myself, felt so inadequate, lacked so greatly in self-esteem, this was the grand-daddy of circumstances.

I graduated M.C. Williams School of Communications with a 4.0 average and National Forensics Society Degree of Distinction. I was named Best Thespian. The journey was nowhere close to being over, but Williams High School Forensics had saved my life. Williams High Forensics was, indeed, groovy! But, in truth, I should have been fucking committed. A student of theatre and communications, in a program designed to nurture, train, and develop those specific abilities, I was unable to say out aloud in mixed company, to someone other than God, that what I wanted most to do in the entire world was entertain, act, dance, live on the stage, and on the screen. For fear that I would again hear the question, "What makes you think …", and still not be able to provide an answer, I hid my dream from the world, and ultimately, from myself.

Introducing, Miss Lorraine Hansberry

Good evening. My name is Lorraine Hansberry. I am a writer. I suppose I think that the greatest gift that man has is art, and I am audacious enough to think of myself as an artist.

To Be Young, Gifted, & Black

Audacious: [aw-day-shuhs], adjective
1. extremely bold or daring; recklessly brave; fearless:
2. extremely original; without restriction to prior ideas;
3. recklessly bold in defiance of convention, propriety, law, or the like; insolent; brazen.
4. lively; unrestrained; uninhibited

Playing the role of Lorraine Hansberry as a senior in High School, in the play, *To Be Young, Gifted, and Black* was crucial to my becoming. It sounded the alarm of my remembrance; it was the first of many, but I heard it.

[Many people like to use the term "awakening" these days, but I also like the concept of remembrance. Perhaps it is an awakening to remembrance, but remembrance, to me, is important. Remembrance implies that there is something we once knew and can know again. Yet, if I were to go with the popular theme of awakening, I'd have to say, in the words of Rev. Albert B. Cleage, Jr., that I did not yet arise, "stretch, wipe the sleep from [my] eyes, look at the world and what it [had] done to [me], and cry out in rage", but my eyes began to open, blinking ever so gently.]

Since being forced to leave M. C. Williams after my 7th grade year to, once again, further the cause of integration, I had not found that same level of theatrical training any place; so, my participation waned. By 9th grade I had given up. I had no other reason to go to school. So, life for me was pretty much the pits. Returning to M. C. Williams for Summer Theatre following my 10th and 11th grade years was nothing less than grace and mercy. Not enough to "keep me all the days of my life", but grace and mercy nonetheless. So, when that literal tap on the shoulder came, summer 1976, it was a god-send. I pretty much withdrew myself from Waltrip HS and enrolled in MCW Magnet School of Communications. It resulted in my having to move in with my sister, Pam, but that was fine with me.

For 99 reasons, at least 76 of them in my head, about 10 of which are listed a couple of pages back, and the rest a result of everything that's been shared about my life up to this point, I actually felt like an oddball upon my return to M.C., but you've read that story. So, I pause primarily to express my deepest gratitude that with every god-send there seems to come a life-line or two.

Accidentally becoming lead dancer in the Christmas show was a life-line. My dance partner did not show up that evening for the performance; so, I had to turn the choreography into a solo; luckily, I was center stage already, and luckily, I had a special lift in one of the routines; so, it worked out perfectly and did a lot for my self-esteem. Being cast as Lorraine Hansberry in our UIL One Act Play was THE life-line of life lines. We did not advance to State and everybody in the cast was very upset. I realized on the bus returning to the school that I was not as angry as the rest, but I was looking at the experience from a totally different perspective. For them, this was about competition. For me, this was about my life. From each of those life-lines, I not only gained confidence in my gifts and talents, with each experience a piece of me awakened, and a piece of me remembered who I had come here to be. Researching the life of Lorraine Hansberry, especially, awakened me to the artist and the activist within me, and I was audacious enough to begin to think of myself as such. Audacious, yes, but it would be several years before audacity, self- confidence, and self-awareness would yawn and stretch and wipe their eyes synchronistically.

And They Called it Puppy Love: II

He cried, real tears. He said he loved me, and confessed that he was afraid I would leave him, go off to college, then to New York someplace and become a famous actress. How well he knew me. That was my dream, having only once crossed my tongue and uttered aloud to ridicule and disbelief, never to part these lips again. How did he know? During the crush years, trying to be impressive, I had told him that I wanted to be a GARnecologist, when I meant to say GYnecologist. Every-body laughed when he corrected me, but, for once, I didn't care about being laughed at because it was a lie anyway. After that, came Journalism and Archeology, but never an actress. So, in true Bogie and Bacall style, I promised I wouldn't leave him, at least not for too long. I'd go to college close by so he could drive up to see me. I mean, I was 17 now, and he was 22. We had created and ended a life together, something that bound us to one another; so, surely, we were destined to be together, forever. Right?

So, that's what I did for love. Dreams already silenced and tucked away were now buried. I buried my dreams and set out for a college I had no interest in attending, to major in a field I had no desire to pursue. With a major in English and minor in Theatre, I decided to become a teacher. To my

credit, I was the first African American to be nominated Outstanding Freshman Woman and was nominated to represent two different academic departments, English and Foreign Language. Each Professor told me I would not win, but they decided I should be nominated. I didn't realize, then, what kind of stance they were taking in 1977, and what kind of statement I was making by accepting the nominations and actually showing up at the banquet.
It was hilarious. A couple of my friends passed the Banquet Hall on campus and saw me sitting at the table with my Professors, the only Black person at this all white affair. I hadn't told anyone I as nominated because I knew I wasn't going to win. One friend kept passing by the window, back and forth, trying to get my attention to find out what kind of revolution I was trying to start. I mean, I was still kinda channeling Lorraine Hansberry; "Am I revolutionary? Intellectually, without a doubt…"

I became, that freshman year, the only African American female on the Dean's list, but was too afraid to go to the swim party at the President's house by myself. As pathetic as that sounds, still, I was blossoming into myself. I knew I was afraid and I admitted it. I had grown tired of being the token Black; I was able to admit to myself also, that I simply did not possess the token Black personality. Alarms were sounding.

Yet, as my path would have it, my hearing became deafened by the sound of wedding bells. College held no interest for me no matter how much I lied to myself and to

Mr. Turner in that long assed letter about becoming an English teacher rather than an actress; so, marriage was the next logical step. I headed home after my freshman year, giving new meaning to, "Stop, in the name of love".

I wasn't in the Houston city limits a good couple of weeks and either I went totally deaf or everything went quiet. Nah, I wasn't deaf; they stopped; the wedding bells just stopped ringing. All that I was not, was thrown in my face by someone I loved and trusted, who had once accepted me as I was. I lost a friend and a piece of myself. I was 18, would be 19 in a couple of months.

PART III

in search of our mothers' gardens

Alice Walker

Ruined

It's the title of a wonderful play, and it clearly expresses what I thought of myself during my college years, Ruined. I casually mentioned before that my senior year of high school I had an abortion. Well, I had a second one my freshman year of college. The technician at the Abortion Clinic cried with me. She kept telling me she couldn't go through with it until she heard me say, "I want to have an abortion." She wouldn't accept the words, "I have to have an abortion". It sounded too much like I was being coerced. All I could say was, "I'm not ready. It was a mistake." When I explained, "I was careful. I've been on the pill for two years, but I throw up after taking it", she cried even harder. I guess she cried for the idiot I was; I had no idea I was also throwing up the pill. I insisted, "My daddy will be so disappointed". She held my hands as I explained how the first abortion happened, how my daddy found out. She was a sister; she reminded me of my eldest sister, Kat. Kat had died during my freshman year, while I was home on Christmas break.

[While I feel the need to stop right here and talk about Kat's death, I'm not sure that this is where it belongs. I wrote a piece awhile back, which I entitled, "Kat". I wrote it at a very defining moment in my life. It was a purging, purifying moment. Perhaps, I will revisit it at the right time and place, get into those feelings, and come to know what Kat had come, that day, to say.]

This Technician, who reminded me of Kat, knew my story, of having lost my mother and been raised by my dad who had made sure his girls had everything they needed, and never had to depend on anybody or anything. I felt her anger rise as I told her how my step-mother, who I discovered was opening the mail my older sister, Joby, sent me from college, was also a frequent snoop through my dresser drawers and had found the pain medication from my first abortion, and decided to share the news with anybody who would listen, including people at church. She had accused me of spreading rumors about my step-sister, rumors I actually had no knowledge of until she brought them up and confirmed them to be true; so, to exact vengeance, she told everybody.

[Okay, I'm just now doing the math. A 46 year old woman exacted vengeance on a 17 year old kid to whom she was supposed to have become mother, seven years earlier. I'm just saying.]

That first time, when the news was spread, Kat came into my room and laid across the foot of my bed and cried because I did not think I could come to her or to Pam, the next eldest, because I had gone through this experience alone. I felt so sorry for her. She just didn't know how estranged I actually felt from my own sisters.

[Yeah, I'm gonna have to share that purge piece to explain why I could not turn to my older sister.]

Daddy had come in and said I pulled a fast one on him; he looked just as sad as Kat. This time, I explained to the Technician, I had to get through it with anybody knowing. If I did, I would ask God for forgiveness. I was about to get married; so, it would never happen again. With the hope of forgiveness and it never happening again, I found a way to say, "I want to get an abortion". I had to.

I was a pretty damned good speaker. I began speaking before the church when I was 12, and won my first Optimist Club Contest against high school students as a 7th grader also; it was third place, but still. In my community of Acres Homes, there just seemed to be a concentration of speaking and acting talent; thus, we had great support from the community. I was often invited to speak for different occasions, especially at churches, which caused me to examine the Bible closely, and to raise questions, lots of questions. I had been part of a Christian girls' group in my church that had the most awesome mentors and sponsors - matrons, as they were called, who earnestly sought to answer my questions and provide me with guidance. I took my charge very seriously, not only the speaking and playwriting, but my Christian journey as a whole, "my walk with the Lord". You know, falling and getting back up again, until the abortions.

After the first, I was ashamed that people knew. My friend

who had also become pregnant, but carried her baby to term, was celebrated. The birth of her son was celebrated. I felt like "a wretch undone", whatever that meant; I had heard the preachers say it.

That reminds me. One young preacher leading the revival that year had called up all the youth to the altar, and was trying his damnedest to get me to say, "I believe I am saved", but, I couldn't say it because I didn't believe it. I had "sinned and come short of the glory of God" and had sense enough to know I'd "sin" again, in fact, sinning was on my agenda for later. Well, that young preacher rolled his eyes, shook his head, took a deep breath, and said, "Let us pray". Then, we all took our seats, whether we believed we were saved, lied to get it over with, refused to lie to get it over with, or just weren't saved at all. I guess I had held up the service long enough. In my defense, he started that charade, not me.

I had begun to question the whole notion of being saved. Never one to go off half-cocked, and definitely not ready to defy everything I had been conditioned to believe about the Lord, though it was beginning to make less and less sense, I decided to "study to shew [my]self, approved unto God, a workman that needeth not to be ashamed, rightly dividing the word of truth.". Besides, that's what we would say every Sunday after Sunday School, in unison, "Study the word; study the word; study the word; 2nd Timothy 2:15". I didn't know then that the King James Bible had been translated in the year 1611, and in the year 1611, the word study meant "strive, or be diligent". As an English major I would later learn that word meanings not only change across languages and translations, but across time periods as well, and I already stated, I was a very literal child. So, I went off to college and found Billy Graham, Cory Ten Boom, Dr. Norman Schuler. Already a voracious reader, I read almost everything they wrote and became correspond-dents with them. I even went off on a retreat with 3-4 car loads of white kids to learn how to study the bible in a year - FYI, not a one of them, not even the instructor said a word to me the whole time I was there. The girl who signed me up wasn't even there. Was I crazy?! Coulda woke up hangin' from a tree! I didn't know it, but I was becoming a "seeker". I didn't know about seeking then; I just knew about being saved, and, well, no amount of Billy Graham was going to save me, especially after the second abortion, especially since the wedding bells had stopped, and there wasn't going to be a wedding to make everything right with God. I was ruined and would just have to stay that way.

19 and Pregnant

  I always say, when things happen that are totally out of your control, that's the work of Spirit, and the experience has come to show you to yourself. When things happen that you clearly created, not through mis-spoken words, conditioned beliefs, or unwitted sponsoring thoughts, but through your own decisive actions, there is a lesson to be learned.

I got pregnant. No, I wasn't still throwing up birth control pills. I had found myself a new form of birth control, but I was out, and I did not listen to that still, small voice, saying, "Girl, get up. Don't trust him." I listened, instead, to that loud mouth who had been drowning everybody out for the last two years. "If you want him back, this is what you have to do. Tonight. You might not get another chance." I listened to his voice. "I wouldn't mind having a little baby with you." This, from the same guy who talked you out of going away to pursue your dreams, who would not even tell his mama he was planning to marry you. He was saying what I wanted to hear. So, I listened, and I heeded. I looked in that drawer one last time, nothing; I bit my lip and slid between the sheets.

The love of my life and I had broken up two months earlier, almost as soon as I had come home from college. I was enrolled in University of Houston and working at the chicken shack to save money for my wedding, when I realized I was the only one talking about marriage. When I asked if he had told his mother, and he said he hadn't, those wedding bells began to sound a lot like alarms and whistles.

So, I was not having sex. I had actually become what would be called today, a stalker. I actually stalked this guy; he never knew it though. Funny stories for another time, like the time I had to back up down a one-way street in downtown Houston so he wouldn't see me driving past his job as he exited the building. So, who needed birth control? Five years older than I, he was finally growing up. I didn't hold a candle to his new friends. I didn't think he would come around again. I didn't think I would invite him to stay. I didn't think I would be so willing to tempt Mother Nature. The lack of self-esteem is a serious bitch!

I was 19 and pregnant; I created that situation. It was my decision. What was I going to learn from it? By the time the pregnancy test was positive, I was abandoned and alone again. That was not my decision, but it was an experience I brought upon myself. It was truly an awakening, and nothing awakens a sleeping giant like having a mouth to feed, having someone else depending on you, having someone else look at you with their eyes full of trust and love, unconditional love, wanting only that in return. Still, awakening, even awakening to remembrance, is a process; it happens in steps and stages for most of us. It doesn't matter that you're now a young mother, a young, single, mother. Life keeps moving; the process of awakening keeps happening. I stumbled. I faltered. I second guessed myself and my own instincts, my mother's intuition. I took the advice of those I thought knew better than I. The top of my closet was a library of books and pamphlets on parenting, but there are just some things that only life experience can teach you when you're just 19, and got a long way to go. I got a lot of things wrong; I got some things right.

Audacious Enough

One thing I got right was moving to Dallas, Texas. I was 24, about to turn 25. The guy I was seeing then was there for grad school at SMU. He had an agent and showed her my picture, told her about my Theatre background. She suggested to him that I move to Dallas; she would represent me. I did. I spent the summer there with him, losing weight, learning the city of Dallas, deciding where to live, checking out the schools, as my five year old, Kam Enita, would be starting Kindergarten. I took time to get out and learn about the film industry, explore the theatre climate. By mid-August, I had found an apartment, and Kam and I made our move.

A teaching job literally fell into my lap. I had gone to Richardson ISD to sign up as a Substitute Teacher, thinking it was too close to the start of school to land a teaching job. Kam and I were in the lobby of the building laughing about all the brochures she had collected when a gentleman bounded down the steps. He looked at us; I was a bit embarrassed as I thought we had gotten a little silly.
He asked. "Do you teach English?" Shocked shitless, I said I did. "Come with me." I was hired to teach English that day. Things were looking great. My last check from Klein school district, where I had taught the year before, was still due, and I had a little money left over from the totally unexpected check I had received from the modeling agency I had attended before leaving Houston. Just before I was to

graduate, they went out of business. I got a portion of my money back. We were gonna be okay.

The agent I signed with called about casting for a play, "You Can't Take it With You". The only role in the play for an African American female was a maid. I told my friend about it; he insisted that no actress in Dallas worth her salt was going to show up for that audition. He named a young lady that he believed to be at the top of her game and at the top of the Black Dallas theatrical scene. She certainly wasn't going to audition for that part. I did a little research and discovered that Marla Gibbs had played the role and it was actually the character that birthed the idea of Florence on "The Jeffersons". I decided I would start paying my own dues, and audition. I got there, scared to death, and not only was the aforementioned actress there, there were many others. I was cast. It was my introduction into professional theatre. Dallas was good to me. I did theatre. I did film. That thing about having no regrets; I take that back. I guess I still have one, leaving Dallas the way I did. It was time, but I took the wrong path. I think.

[I had a dream a few years ago that I was flying over a building, a huge barn where Black people were fighting each other for some reason. I asked myself, where I should go. "Back to Dallas" was the answer that came out of the sky, but I do not interpret dreams literally. Dallas symbolized the mindset and who I had become as a result of being and having been there. The dream was urging me back to that state of being.]

Dallas was good to me. It was there that I established myself as an actress, model, and choreographer.

On the set of my first film shoot, *The Fig Tree,* shot in Waxahachie, TX, a short distance from Dallas.

I had a trailer with my name on it.

 Even got three of my nephews in on the project, Geryl, Corey, and Hise. My kid was having a blast. I could get used to this.

I was working with and learning from veteran actors like …

Olivia Cole, who won an Emmy for the role of Mathilda, wife of Chicken George, in the *Roots* miniseries, and Teresa Wright, Oscar winner from the old studio days, known for challenging the Studio System.

Kam and Jared, my nephew, were queen and king of photo opps.

With Tony Randall on the set of *Save the Dog*, my second film project. Kam kept calling him Mr. Randalls. I worked with Cyndy Williams of *Laverne and Shirley* on that project as well.

From sharecropper to security guard, I was paying my dues. My next role would be as prison inmate, Elvira, in *Chained Heat*, which featured my favorite actress, Loretta Devine, not just because she's my home girl and a distant relative, but she's a damned good actress. There were print jobs and a couple of commercials.

Dallas also introduced me to the world of pageantry.

Miss Black Dallas, 1986

Miss Black America
1st Runner-Up,
1987

Ms. Black Texas,
1991
Metroplex System

Ms. Black USA,
1992
Metroplex System

[Ah-mazing! As I think back on it, that whole pageant period was period of metamorphosis.]

The one person I should have been able to depend on to support me as I embarked on that journey, did not even believe I could win, and made no bones of telling me so. Still, I felt in my Spirit that I could. By the time of the pageant, he had moved out of state. When I called to tell him, I said; "Guess who won the Miss Black Dallas Pageant?"

His answer. "Who?"

Yes, I am rolling on the floor laughing my fat ass off right now, but in 1986, I was not. It was a red flag. You need to drop this negro like an STD; he does not believe in you, but he wants you to believe in him. It's time for you to believe in yourself with no approval or validation from others. After a few months, I did.

Miss Black Dallas, Miss Black America - 1st Runner-Up, Ms. Black Texas, Ms. Black USA ... what I had hoped to gain from it all was an opportunity to meet people who might help further my career as an actress, to gain exposure, but more than anything, the experience was drawn to me that I might begin to develop the confidence in myself to actually meet people, introduce myself, and believe that I was worth their time. The test came during my Ms. Black USA reign, the title I ended up resigning, on the same morning I was supposed to have breakfast with then President, Bill Clinton, along with 100's of other people of course. It was a matter of principle.

[Spoiler alert: This pageant win, the USA win, actually occurred after I had left Dallas and returned to Houston to live, but I credit Dallas with planting the seed. Yep, I left the Big D and ended up back in Houston. It wasn't a straight shot, but I'll get back to the main story in a second. I need to explore this pageantry experience. Walk with me for a minute.]

As Ms. Black USA (Metroplex System), I had been asked to make an appearance and speak at a program for elementary school girls. I shared the information with the individual responsible for my bookings. Unfortunately, in an effort to get me to choose Bill Clinton over the girls, misinformation was shared. It had happened before. There had been other incidents and sharings of misinformation that I had tolerated and smiled through. This would be the end of it. I stood in my truth, and said, "Enough".

I had begun to take the necessary steps toward even recognizing my truth while in Los Angeles. As Ms. Black USA, I had gone to Los Angeles to attend a tribute to Clarence Avant being given by Quincy Jones. Everybody in Black entertainment was there. I wondered how in the world I would be able to take advantage of this opportunity. What would I do? What would I say? I didn't have time for rubbing elbows and hob-knobbing. I was not an autograph hound; so, I'd have to make this thing work for me. How would I not seem desperate? How forward would I have to be? The founder of the Pageant System happened to have a very handsome, young son living in L.A. Before the event, he told me he would be my escort and would ensure that I met everybody possible.

[I knowed there was a God ... in my Sophia Jane voice.]

He did just that, and each time he did, I very graciously attempted to seize the opportunity to make a lasting contact without screaming, "I'm an actress; I can write; hire me!" Unfortunately, when I returned home and followed up on a couple of leads, nothing panned out. It had been a nice evening, a great experience. I experienced being on a red carpet and having the media yell my name so I could turn around and get snapped; bulbs were flashing everywhere. I rubbed elbows, and got tons of compliments, yada yada yada.

While, at first, I thought no one took me seriously because I had a big crown on my head and, perhaps, they assumed I was a beauty with no brain or talent, I remembered Vanessa Williams whose career was bolstered by her beauty pageant win, and scandal. I had a revelation. Confirmation of this revelation came much later while I was at the Hollywood Black Film Festival, where an ugly rumor about Black entertainers who had "made it" proved to be an unfortunate truth.

As we excitedly shuffled from one seminar/ panel/ workshop/presentation to the next, the rumor was that Black people don't want to help other Black people get a foot in the door. It was being rumored that none of these Black celebs would help us; we'd have to figure out how to make our own way. The truth was, they acted like they were going to help; they gave you cards and told you to submit here, submit there; but, only a few Black entertainers were in a position to help anybody do anything. They could only think of themselves, how to stay relevant, and get to the next gig. I understood it, and realized that had been the case at the Quincy Jones affair.

At least one guy pretended to be interested and made me promise not to forget him (I could use an emoji right here), and Queen Latifah just came on out and said that scripts for "Living Single" had to be submitted via representation to the Executive Producer, just make sure my representation is reputable. I got it. She probably had tons of writers asking her to read their stuff every day. Debbie Allen stared at me strangely while handing me her card; Wesley Snipes thought it cute to adjust my crown. I clearly understood that of the few who can, or could at that time in Black Hollywood history, there are even fewer who will keep their foot in the door once it opens for them. The point of all this is that the pageantry experiences, did, indeed serve my metamorphosis into a woman of confidence with belief in myself and my abilities. The Black Hollywood experience as I like to call it brought me to the realization that in whatever form I desired my career to manifest, it would be totally up to me. Neither pageants nor appearances nor elbow rubbing would do the trick. It wasn't about knocking on doors or beating the pavement. It was a hard pill to swallow; it took a minute to get into my system, but I got it.

Mine was never intended to be the journey of a thousand no's to the one, great, yes. I am the yes I am looking for.

So, yes, Dallas had been good to me. I went there to get my feet wet in the industry and, indeed, it was my introduction to many things, especially myself. I was so in awe of my friends who had braved moves to L.A. and New York to pursue their careers, who just jumped in with both feet. One friend, when she returned home for a visit, I asked a thousand questions. She, unfortunately, and as is par for my course, took my questioning the wrong way. She thought I was fishing to see if she was actually working and pursuing her career; besides, there were some other dynamics at play that night of which I was not a part and she thought I was. I truly admired her for making that move. I often wondered where I would be if I had gone to the college I really wanted to attend, if I had moved to L.A. or New York instead of Dallas, if I stuck to my plan and moved to L.A. after Dallas.

[If you're reading these words, old friend, please know that it was nothing more than admiration that fueled my inquiries, that, and nothing more.]

One night in Dallas, on the floor of my living room, assessing the strides I had been able to make in my career thus far. I got lost in the "what if's", and remembered how my sister, Kat, had urged me to go away, to pursue my dreams. I realized she had been the only one to do so. I held some very painful feelings about Kat, and they began to weigh very heavily upon me. I decided that if I wrote them out, perhaps I could come to terms with those feelings. Kam was in Houston, visiting family for the summer; so, I wrote all day and into the night. I had baked a strawberry cake a day or two before. I ate cake for breakfast, lunch, and dinner. I ate cake through the laughter. I ate cake through the tears. Lying on the floor in the fetal position, sobbing, I comforted myself with strawberry cake. By the end of the night, I guess I had begun to channel Lorraine Hansberry again. I wrote on a little note to self:

" The greatest gift that man has is art, and I am audacious enough to think of myself as an artist.
I am a writer. I am going to write."

"Remembering Kat"
(written July, 1986)

In the words of the infamous, immortal Kat, Kathlynn Dianne Westmoreland Thomas Jenkins, "Jump Judy! Cut high or stay at home; cut high or stay at home." Amazing! The same domino or card playing tirade which instilled fear in my childhood heart and is the reason I never became adept at either game, has become words of such profundity to me now, 25, having just stepped out into life. It was a metaphor for life. "Cut high, or stay at home." Rarely though, do we take our own medicine, or maybe it just seems that way to those on the outside, looking in.

"What chu fishin' fuh?" Kat would ask any opponent brave or stupid enough to join her in a friendly game. "You ain't got nothin'. All the sixes gone; your pahtnuh got the last of the deuces, and I'm holding you over here baby. I'm holding you over here. So, play! Play!" Climbing on top of the table, "See there! See there!" Slamming her domino or card on the table with every word, "I - tol'- you - to - stay - at- home. Bam! Get up! Next!"

Kat must've spent all of her time at PV playing cards and dominoes, because she did not pass one class the whole time she was there, well not enough to stay and see it through. From what I understand, Daddy made Kat come home after her first year. With her, came cussin, dirty dishes, and dirty clothes. Soon, she had a following of two, Joby and me, the prodigal children. Pam had done her best. She had become our overseer when Mama died and Kat when off to PV. We still talk about that time Daddy fussed about the rice being burned, and she cried; so, Joby cried, and Daddy looked like he wanted to cry, and even at the age of seven I knew it wasn't about the rice. Though I have memories of teaming up with Kat against Pam and Joby to see who could get their share of the house cleaned before Mama came home, and in wrestling matches against Pam and Joby, there were eleven or twelve years between Kat and me, too much time, too much space, too much life.

There was the time she threw and hit me in the head with a shoe because I wouldn't sit still in front of the t.v., causing a huge hickey to rise on my forehead, and the time she tried to act like Mama and pinch me for throwing pancakes in the trash. She actually made me get the pancakes out of the trash and eat them; claimed she was teaching me a lesson about being wasteful and cooking too much. There were the Saturday mornings Joby and I got up expecting to watch Saturday morning television, to find that Kat had rolled the t.v. into the bathroom. We would stand outside the door banging, yelling for her to release the t.v., and Pam would give a loud wail, "Uuuggghhh, Kathyyy! Gimme the phone!" Yeah, Kathy would stretch the phone cord into the bathroom as well, laughing as the three of us shouted from the other side. The first time it happened, we simply crawled into the bathroom through the dirty clothes hamper which opened into Daddy's bathroom as well as ours. Would you believe Kat started blocking the hamper with a chair so we couldn't get through?!

Before Kat came home, Joby and I never cursed or talked back or wasted things. We ate what was cooked and didn't complain. Then Kat came home. "Tell her she can't tell you what to do." Joby and I echoed. "You can't tell us what to do." I guess Pam just gave up, and decided to just let Kat be the big sister, bad influence though she was. It seems like that's when things started happening so extremely, unbelievably fast. It was like I looked away from the t.v. one day and Joby was crying because the rumor amongst her friends' older siblings about Pam being pregnant was true; Pam was married; Daddy had married Ms. Robison, my second grade teacher; Kat had cursed out Ms. Robison's sister and moved away; Jobbie had turned 13, and life as we knew it was over.

Kat did return home for a while. Our grandmother, Mama Josephine, was visiting from Louisiana. Kat would sleep all the time. Mama Josephine said, "Ya know, beby, ah b'lieve Kat must be tekkin dem dopes, yeh." Kat wasn't on drugs; Kat was pregnant, and before we knew it, she was throwing up against the wall. Pam was running back and forth with wet towels; Joby and Deirdre, our step-sister, a year older than Joby, were calling folks up on the phone, and I stood back watching the whole thing play out like a B movie. Kat came home with the ugliest creature I had ever seen, unlike Pam's baby, who was a pretty little girl. Kat gave that baby three middle names, Christopher Jo Eric LaMarque

Thomas, but for a while, we called him Fish. That's what he looked like. Then came Jemiel, who looked just like Fish did, ugly. I was 11 and honest; those babies were ugly. I said it, and each time, I got a good cursing out. I take responsibility for naming Jemiel. It was the era of the Jackson 5 and Deirdre was in love with Jermaine. Jobbie must have been in love with Tito, whose real name was Toriano, because she kept saying, "Name him Tito. Name him Tito", but Kat said, "What the hell kind of name is Tito?" Well, I was in love with Michael Jackson and Donny Osmond. Poor Michael, if he had just married me when we were eleven, he might be alright today, might still be Black. Unfortunately, every-body's name was Michael, and Donny was a goofy white boy as far as Kat was concerned; so, I said, "Be original. Name him Jemiel." She did, Jemiel Toriano Thomas.

Kat's wedding was in the den. I don't even remember getting dressed up for it. I have often wondered why nobody told me to put on some clothes for Kat's wedding. I've so often, since then, felt that I dishonored my sister, like her life was not meaningful to me. I'm not the most affectionate person in the world, I know that. I have vivid recollections of being told by my mother after returning home from a trip, "Hug your sister", and being told by my Dad when he returned from a trip, "You're supposed to hug a person you haven't seen in a while." The last thing I want to live with is that I didn't show my sister any sisterly love at all before she left this earth. I just don't understand what could have been going through my head that I wasn't dressed for the occasion. Was it unannounced, a spur of the moment thing? Somebody had to know; it was at the house; she and Pam wore similar dresses, I think. There was a preacher. There was food; I think. I don't remember a lot. I don't remember enough, except that I was standing there in the doorway, looking like something the cat dragged in. I was looking at the Best Man who had been my Godfather and I heard the preacher say, "Do you, Kathlynn Diane Westmoreland ..." Westmoreland? Why did he say Westmoreland? It's Thomas, Kathy Thomas, my big sister. I searched the room for other faces to look as confused as mine. I searched the room for faces with answers, clues, nothing. Until, one day, we were getting on I-45, right out of downtown, and Ms. Robison (we still called her that even after she married Daddy), decided she would take it upon herself to inform me that "Kathy is not Joe's child anyway; your mama had Kathy before she met Joe."

Who would have known, except that we didn't have Kat's fire, that impulse, that zest for life, that passion for a good card game. Daddy never differentiated between Kat and us, nor us and Deirdre. That must've been a step-mother thing; differentiating between whose kids were whose must've been part of the step-mother's creed or code. If it was, Ms. Robison deserved a certificate of participation and a medal for exemplary compliance.

Fortunately, the news that Kat was not my father's child would mean nothing to me but a bit of family history to be explored. While I take deeply, regretful ownership for the distance I later felt between Kat and me, in my defense, I was a kid. There were eleven or twelve years between us and life was happening. That distance was not immediately apparent. By the time I realized it, it was too late.

I remember being at church one Sunday, and coming out at the end of service to find Kat there. It was as if I had not seen her in ages, didn't know who she was. I went up to her, and in the true fashion of my mental conditioning, questioned everything from her choice of blouse, to the stain on my nephew's blanket, and the worn out shoes on her feet. I heard the same judgement, belittlement, and degradation in my voice that I heard and felt on a daily basis, and was terrified, ashamed, and sorry. Had I not heard myself, God only knows what other persona might have taken residence in my psyche, and in the words of Dan Akyroyd (Ghostbusters), "It sounds like you've got at least two or three people in there already".

Thank God, I heard myself, but the damage was done, and the worst was not that I had developed into a hyper critical individual of myself and others, but it kept me from hearing my big sister when she said my boyfriend was too old for me; I couldn't feel her sadness and big sister guilt when she found out I had gotten pregnant and couldn't come to her, and had gone through an abortion my senior year of high school alone. I gave no value to her advice that I go away to college and follow my dreams. "With your grades and SAT scores, you can go anywhere." I really did want to go to New York, or Carnegie Mellon, or somewhere in that direction, but other voices had my ear. The one person who offered me the encouragement I needed had been discredited in my eyes long ago. What did she know? Three kids, different daddies, home, attire, education, career, none to the standard of my mental conditioner. In my eyes, my big sister had been diminished. So, I went up to Wichita Falls, and when I came home for Christmas, Kat died on me.

She had fallen ill, thought it was the flu. Unable to get out and do anything, she let me use her car to get around and hang out with my friends. Every time you turned left, the horn would blow. So, we would wave at whoever responded to the sound of the horn. I had gotten together with some theatre friends to go see a movie. We picked up our former theatre teacher, Mr. Turner. Every time I turned left, the horn blew, and we waved. Mr. Turner said, "Lord, y'all know everybody in Acres Homes". We all died laughing, secretly deciding to keep up the charade, at least until we were turning into the parking lot of the Garden Oaks movie theatre and there was no one to wave to. I don't know if it was that night or the next, but Kat was rushed to hospital.

It was like a scene out of a movie. They had discovered she didn't have the flu, but fluid around her heart. I went in where she was and the doctors were all around her. So, I backed away. I heard a sound. I couldn't tell if she was calling my name or moaning in pain. I ran outside. It was a small hospital and my escape was just a few feet away. I have wondered since that day if she saw me, if she called out to me. I have wondered if I hadn't run out, if I could have helped her fight for her life.

Daddy brought Chris and Jemiel to the hospital, but it was too late. Joby grabbed them in the parking lot and squeezed them so. When my brain finally processed what had happened, I ran past and grabbed up a hand full of rocks and started throwing them, something I probably saw on t.v. That's where I learned to deal with life, t.v. Whenever something tragic happens, just go off by yourself and throw rocks. What else was I supposed to do, stand there looking, and watch my sister die? I guess they hadn't started making movies yet, where people go in, sit down, take the hand of their loved one, and hold it, until, because I didn't think of that. I didn't think of that. I didn't think of that, shit! I wasn't there for my sister when she needed me most. It's one thing to fuck up in life, say I'm sorry, and do what you can to fix it. It's a whole nother party when you don't know if you fucked up, there's nobody to tell you what really happened, no opportunity to say I'm sorry and fix it. So, you carry that shit around with you for the rest of your life. Did my sister call for me? That's all I want to know, but I'll never know.

At the cemetery, I heard these long, loud sobs, and I couldn't tell where they were coming from. I just hoped they were mine. Lord, please let them be mine. Please let me cry for my sister; the least I could do was cry for my sister. I could feel somebody lifting me up, but something was telling me not to move; so, I couldn't move. I couldn't leave Kat there, not this time. This time, I was not going to run away; I had to stay there with her, with my big sister. Somebody stronger than I lifted me up, and led me to the car. When I got inside, Joby folded over onto Pam. Pam folded over onto me. I pushed her hair back and wiped her face, then turned to look out of the window. For the first time in my life, I saw my daddy cry. He doubled over the car, and cried. I wanted to reach through the window and hold him too, but he saw me looking at him, saw the tears welling up in my eyes, pulled himself together, and shook his head, no. So, I sucked mine up too; I pushed them back; I pushed those tears way back. Daddy got in the front seat of the car. Pam's head lay on my shoulder; Joby's lay on hers. Kat was gone from us. Forgive me Kat. I was 18.

Living LaVida Single Mom

> # Do you love me?
> ## Yes or No
> ### Circle

Possibly the worst feeling a mother can have, right after losing a child or watching helplessly as a child suffers, is having a child send you this message: Do you love me? Yes or No, circle. I still well up. Not for myself, but for the child who wrote it, and for the young woman who had to come to the realization that her child did not know that she was loved. Unfortunately, when a sleeping giant awakens, long before she begins to remember that she's a giant, she remembers the hopes, dreams, and aspirations she once buried, but she doesn't awaken with a handbook on how to resurrect and balance them with raising a little one.

I had moved to Chicago, and had been there three or four months when I got the letter. I had planned to take Kam with me, had found just the right apartment near Loyola University. Everyone said the nearby elementary school was pretty good, and there was an all girls' school that I also had my eye on should we make Chicago our home for a minute, though my sights were really on Los Angeles. I was advised against taking her to Chicago with me at first, was told it might be best to go and get myself settled in, then send for her. I didn't want to make a mistake where Kam was concerned; so, I followed that advice. I had no idea it had been influenced by ulterior motives.

Kam was eight years old, starting 3rd grade. I had previously spent 3 months away from her while doing shows at the Youngstown Playhouse, Youngstown, Ohio. While there, my creative partner suggested we check out Chicago for a while; there were good connections there to be made. So, I reasoned, a brief stint in Chicago wouldn't be so bad; exposure to a new place would be good for Kam, and ready her for the transition to L. A., get her used to being a little bit farther from Houston, a little farther away from family than we had been before. Dallas had been good to us, but, it was time to move on.

[May I repeat for emphasis? Giants awaken, but don't fully remember they're giants until they stand.]

I called home each week, but I rarely talked to Kam. I spoke mainly to my sister to make sure everything was okay. I felt guilty for leaving her, and believe it or not, I never knew what to say. If I talked to her for any length of time, there might be questions, well, A question, THE question. Why didn't you take me with you? I would have to answer, and I think I feared the answer more than the question. I would have to say, "Everybody said I shouldn't". Even I knew that was a bullshit answer. I was the mommy. How does the mommy tell her child that somebody else told her what to do? You mean the mommy can't make her own decisions? Why should a kid trust a mommy who can't make her own decisions? I would have to confess that I didn't believe in myself enough to follow my gut. My gut said this kid will not fall apart if she moves a couple of times in life. My gut said, it will be great for her. My gut said she's your kid. She will see you strive for something you want and learn from that. So, I ran from the question I did not want to answer, and I got the worst question I believe a mother can receive and a child can ask, a question a child should never have to ask her mother, a question I never would have imagined being asked. Do you love me, yes or no?

I'm Coming Out

Well, I would've if they'd given me the chance. A good little Baptist girl from the South doesn't just wake up one day in 1986 and decide to be a lesbian or any other non-gender, non-sexuality specific being. She struggles with the notion. Hell, she will have struggled her whole life with it, wondering what it was, especially after innocently that pretty little light skinned girl with the long hair between the sheets hanging on the line. She was 8 or 9, maybe this girl was 10, but no more. The sheets were there. They played, ran in and out, bumped into each other, touched, smiled, kissed, on the lips. She would be convinced later in life that it was just natural childhood sexual exploration, or the handiwork of the devil. If it had been even talked about among church people, except in secrecy and condemning whispers, the latter is what she would've heard. She struggles with the word. It fits, but it doesn't fit. She realizes this is not the sum total of who she is; so, she struggles to find the right words that actually describe who and what she is. If she's awakening and remembering, she has already begun to question the religious dogma that has rendered her a demon seed though she knows she's good at heart and doesn't have "a reprobate mind" no matter what the preacher says. Finally, she would choose to assume full responsibility for where her soul ultimately resides, and sit up late at night writing the words, looking at them from all angles: bull dagger, homosexual, bi-sexual, a-sexual, lesbian, butch, femme, same-gender loving person, androgynous even, a well-balanced yin and yang. She's figured out when she's about thirteen that she definitely doesn't want to be called a bull dagger. Hell, she doesn't want to be called any of these things, even one of those that doesn't sound so bad; but, those who don't choose are labeled sell-outs, accused of being confused. If you don't choose, you don't belong, and God knows she's had her fill of not belonging. So, with the help of Alice Walker, she comes to terms with it, and chooses...

lesbian until further notice.

Unlike Susan (Laura Dern) on the show "Ellen", who received a toaster from Melissa Etheridge when Ellen came out, addressing the myth that lesbians recruit women into lesbianism and get rewarded for it, there was nobody to receive a toaster for recruiting me to the same-gender loving community. Unlike Ellen, nobody signed me up. Melissa Etheridge didn't stamp my gay membership papers; I didn't suddenly belong. In fact, it's a known fact that the gay community could be pretty racist and the Black gay community is busy fighting for inclusion or hiding under the piano benches and in the robe closets at church. So, it was a self-awareness I would have to experience alone, from the inside out; it would cause me to really wonder now. Who am I? What else is lurking under the layers? What do I believe? What is this life of mine all about? Attempts to fix me and save me ranged from ridicule to trickery, accusation to condemnation, and meetings with the preacher.

My stint in Youngstown, Ohio was over; I had gone there to choreograph "Ain't Misbehavin'" and perform in the show "Split Second" at the Youngstown Playhouse. It was my plan to return home, celebrate Kam's birthday, wait out school to be over, then move with her to Chicago. I was in my first lesbian relationship; it was rocky and pretty much at an end less than 6 months after it began, but we remained creative partners, working together as Director/Choreographer. Our Youngstown experience had been very successful, and we were hopeful that we could generate more work together, especially in Chicago where she said she had a few connections. It was also the first time that I actually realized the extent of my talent, and the depth of knowledge and skills in my craft I possessed. Though I had, during this time, grown anxious to face and overcome doubts and fears I recognized in myself, it would be a few more years before awareness of my talent and skill level would inform my confidence and my approach to my career. Besides, I had bigger fish to fry.

I hadn't had the opportunity to "come out" to my family. So, I thought that returning to Houston from Ohio, before heading off to Chicago was the best time to do it; my friend would be traveling home with me, as she had in the past, to help me pull off the birthday party of the century. We were staying at my sister's apartment. She had been married only seven or eight months and my step-mother didn't think we should be encroaching upon the newlyweds. She was finally right about something; so, we began to try and figure out where we would stay for this brief period. My friend was only supposed to be there, I guess, another week; so, we went to my parents' house. During the transition, my sister found my journal, read it, and photocopied those pages that contained my thoughts and feelings about being in a same-gender relationship. It was a journal; it was personal; I have always felt free when writing; so, imagine the explicit nature of the content. After moving to my parents' house for the remainder of the stay, I discovered that my step-mother had begun doing the same, reading through my journal.

A few days passed and I was invited to go jogging with my sister. When I left, my step-mother and elder sister accosted my friend at the house, purchased her an airline ticket, threatened to call her parents and share with them the sordid details of my journal, totally unaware that she had come out to her parents years before we ever even met. Operation outing was in full effect and I was none the wiser. Under the guise of going for a jog, and stopping by my dad's barbershop for a visit, a visit he soon realized I had no knowledge of, a visit that made him very uncomfortable, I was outed to my dad. It actually took me a few minutes to realize what was taking place.

"You judge other people's children, like that boy, and you never even think about your own."

He mentioned the boy's last name, but I won't. It was barely audible, but it was something to that effect. When I looked at him thoroughly confused, he realized I had been set up, that we both had been set up.

"You don't know what I'm talking about do you?"

I shook my head, no. "Unh unh." Then I realized whose last name he had said. It was the name of one of my friends who was an out, gay, male, and it finally hit me. I hadn't yet evolved to grown-up conversations with my Dad. I was about 27, and, on top of that, I was going against the grain, against the norm, and he was my daddy.

[In retrospect, what was so crazy, was that it never even occurred to me that my sexuality was going to be such an issue. It was an issue for me because it caused me to seek greater understanding about who I was and what I believed, but I really didn't think that hard about what it meant to anybody else. I didn't dread coming out. I didn't agonize over it. I thought it would be just a matter of telling them and moving on. Each time I have thought back to this experience, I have asked myself. What the fuck was I thinking?! I brought my girlfriend around my family, to my sister's wedding, to help with my daughter's birthday party. We worked together; we were trying to establish a business together. I wasn't trying to keep it a secret. I knew it was something worth sharing with my family and I intended to do so, but I really didn't make it a big deal. I guess I didn't know enough gay people, or hadn't heard enough coming out stories to realize just how ugly these things could get. I was totally naïve. In thinking back on this experience, I have been able to present myself with two possibilities. Either I believed that my father and my sisters loved me enough to accept me as I was (my step-mother's opinion of me totally did not matter to me by that time of my life), or I presumed that since little to no interest was taken in my life as a teen, no one would care what I did as an adult, and I was an adult. I knew that my father and my sisters loved me. Love has never been the question here. This is about all of the feelings that have affected how I perceived myself, my microcosm, and my relationship to it. Unloved, was never one of those feelings. So, thinking that they loved me enough to not judge me based on my sexuality could certainly be one of the two reasons I really did not realize it was going to affect them the way it did. That, or the perception that they just did not care. I'm sorry, as a manner of speaking, but during my teen years, I did not think anyone cared what the hell I did or what I was going through. So, again, why would they care once I became an adult?]

So, the day of the outing, when my father's tone grew serious, I expected to be questioned about my finances or not using that college degree that so many other people wished they had. That was typically the extent of our "serious" conversation. I had no idea that I was being outed.

[Out, what a word, what symbolism, how true to form, how

par for the course of my life, now that I think about it, now that I'm examining my life. The spine of my life drama had been feelings of alienation, rejection, and insignificance, of feeling out. Well, little did I know, I would be out, in the true sense of the word, in more ways than one. How divine is that?]

I have no remembrance of the conversation with my father or whether or not there was conversation after the moment I realized I was being outed, and we both realized we had been set up. I don't remember if my sister and I spoke as we drove back to my parents' house. I just remember returning to my parents' home and feeling incredibly sorry for my friend. I knew that if I had been set up, there was no telling what had happened to her. We drove to the airport, mainly just to talk. She had no intention of getting on the airplane, if only just to show my family they had no control over her; she had paid her outing dues and was not about to pay mine. She was a grown woman who had come to Houston on her own and would leave on her own. She could be put out of their house, but not out of the city. She had to make that statement, and I fully understood. In fact, I respected that. We seized the opportunity to talk about our relationship, finally verbalizing that it had been over for quite some time, but we were friends, would remain creative partners, and friends.

During that period of waiting for school to be out so that I could make the next move to Chicago, my Dad advised that I not take Kam just yet. It was the first time we'd be that far away from home; I should wait until I was settled in. It seemed like sound advice. It was the worst advice I ever followed, and how short sighted of me that I didn't realize it was directly related to the fact that I was now, out.

Cut High or Stay at Home
Checkin'-In

My feelings about the outing are not about the boldness of disrespect, the self-righteous indignation, the notion that a person can simply tell another how to live her life, imposing beliefs and opinions on another. I'm not feeling some kind of way about the rumors that circulated within my community circle, rumors that I had gone off to Chicago, "chasing behind a woman", much like the rumors when I moved to Dallas; that I had gone off to Dallas "chasing behind a man", rather than seeking career opportunity. It's not about the rumors that I had abandoned my daughter, chasing a dream. Chile, it's not even about the friends who turned their backs on me, who began to read something extra into every word I said to them, who now accused me of coming on to them, or the letters filled with judgement and accusation. I realized long ago that not a one of these people, neither blood nor bond, even knew who the hell I was, before I was outed. Ask them about the girl who jerked off all the guys on the dance floor and was left standing alone with no way home. I'll wait.

CUE: crickets.

What these feelings are about today, in a whole new century, is the realization that the ability to love and accept myself, to go inside and commune with that awakening giant and remember who I was and who I AM, was with me all the time. In the words of Whitney Houston, "I didn't know my own strength." I could have changed my mind, drove those 17 hours back to Houston and snatched my child from the jaws of ignorance, blind religion, and self-righteousness at any moment. I could have stood up for her and for myself, but I didn't. The source of my pissosity is that I did not. I didn't know how to fight for my child and for myself. I am pissed at myself, but I am also enlightened.

"Jump, Judy! Cut high or stay at home." I can hear Kat's voice, and that's what I should have done, cut high, but I didn't. I didn't because I didn't matter; my feelings didn't matter not even to me. I can't even count how many times in life I have been told, tongue in cheek, when attempting to express my feelings, "You know, you're a great actress." So, my feelings were never real. Okay, "never" is much, but too many times, the expression of my feelings was dismissed as great acting. They weren't real. Shit, I wasn't real. Don't forget, I've been a ghost in my lifetime. I had subconsciously accepted that as my reality, my truth.
The message: Cut high! Bet on yourself. Cut high! Trust yourself, your gut, your instinct, your mother's intuition. Cut high! Stand up and realize that you're a giant. Cut high! Be the giant that you are!

The true confession: When I relocated to Chicago and left Kam behind, those times I would call home and not ask to speak with her, wasn't only because I feared the questions

she would ask, but, truth is, I didn't think I really mattered to her. I was of no consequence to anyone; so why would I matter to a kid? I had no mother; mothers were obviously over-rated. I believe what I'm talking about here is "connection". I did not feel a true connection to anyone.
So, no, I did not realize that I was the single most important person in my child's life ... not until I got the letter. This is not about her, but about my perception of myself. I did not matter.

Let me connect some dots. They may seem insignificant, but they help to explain what was at the essence of my being, who I had been and who I had become.
This was a woman who ...

    a. didn't send out high school graduation invitations because she didn't think anybody would bother to come, and didn't have a soul encourage her to do so. A Deaconess and Sunday School Teacher at church, who was also a school Principal, said to me, "I'm not giving you a graduation gift because you didn't give me an invitation; I only give gifts to those who send me an invitation". As she got into her car, I tried to respond. "I didn't order any invitations; I didn't think anybody would come to my graduation". She waved me off; even she, charged with developing young minds, missed the point.

    b. left the throw-away camera in the car at her college graduation, hoping someone would pick it up, afraid

to ask somebody to take pictures for her, afraid her own family would say, "Who do you think you are that someone wants to take pictures of you?"
c. gave herself a college graduation party, hoping to be celebrated in the same manner that her sister had been celebrated when she graduated from college and a dinner party was given for her, but to which the 9 people who showed up, walked in the door with excuses as to why they could not stay.

I know this is old stuff, but that's the point. This shit has history. Where would the thought that I mattered come from? How could I cut high after years of putting my trump card out there only to discover that the game had changed? How could I stay at home? Where was home? Where did I belong? Where did I matter? Where was I free to live the highest expression of myself?

Tapping the Power Within

Face down, arms and legs akimbo, I prostrated myself before the God of my upbringing. Nothing was making sense. The scriptures read like mumbo-jumbo. Not that I didn't understand what I was reading, but what I was reading seemed to no longer require faith, just downright stupidity. Then, there was my southern Baptist upbringing telling me that it "wasn't nothin' but the devil". This is not intended as an insult to those who find strength in religion and direction in the Bible; this was my experience and how I felt about it, what I thought about it. I loved my church, meaning, the people in it. I had grown up with them; my child was growing up there, but I knew it was time to go. So, there I was, begging to be shown the truth, from the only source I believed could be trusted to tell me the truth, the whole truth, and nothing but the truth. Whoever was out there that started this whole mess was the only one who could help me understand it.

Several months later, after a few Sundays of visiting other churches, a few Sundays of sleeping in, even more Sundays at I-Hop, we found ourselves visiting the Shrines of the Black Madonna. Church on Sunday is what you did; so, I set out to find another church. Either I wasn't crazy after all, or we were all crazy. All the things I was reading between the lines of scripture were being spoken, and they made sense. My new partner, Angela, Kam, and I joined the church. It took Kam a minute to adjust to the transition. She was about 12; so, her friends were at our former church; she didn't really want to leave. Eventually, like us, she threw herself into it. The young ladies of her age group became her sisters. With a sincere commitment to give service to God and community, to discover my inner divinity and be all that God created me to be, "I told Jesus, it would be alright, if he changed my name."

I became Raawiya Mwenekweli Obike (storyteller, who brings truth, of a strong household). Angela became Mayasa Osayomwabo Obike (she walks proudly, God will guide her, of a strong household). Kam became Ishaaqa Kamilyah Obike (she loves laughter; she is perfect, of a strong household). Reconnecting with our African heritage was a part of putting off the ego self and making the journey inward to the authentic self, the Christ self. Some people totally renounced their "slave" names; we did not. Outside the church, particularly in business, I used my birth name. I knew my family history with regard to how we got the Thomas name, and I wanted to honor my great grandmother's experience, not write it off.

I was standing in the Shrine Bookstore and Cultural Center which was the outreach arm of the church, where Black books and cards, African artifacts, Black art and collectibles, cultural clothing, gifts, and what-nots were and still are sold. African History, Contemporary Black Reality, Swahili, and other classes were taught. It was and still is home to the African Holocaust Exhibit. I was in that affirming, uplifting, inspiring environment, perusing titles when the book, <u>Tapping the Power Within</u> literally fell off the shelf. I looked around to see if anybody else had witnessed it. Feeling the energy in the room, I took it as a sign that I needed to read it. I had only heard of Iyanla Vanzant, but she and Deepak Chopra were referenced quite a bit by a sister in my Basic Training Group; so, when the book hit the floor, after looking around for the spirit of an ancestor, I picked it up, thumbed through it, and bought it. It set me on a new path toward a new way of thinking and being.

Being at the Shrine was a blessing and a curse at the same time. It was the bridge that crossed me over. The wisdom, knowledge, and understanding that were being propagated at the Shrine was unmatched, unparalleled by any Black church, any Black institution for that matter. People filled the church on Sundays, just as I had, seeking Spiritual truth, truth being the answer to why their personal stories and the story of us as a soul group, as a people, did not fit within the framework of the religiosity of our upbringing. The Cultural Center and Book Store teemed with people on Wednesday evenings and Saturdays, all seeking the truth about their history and heritage beyond the typical Black History Month citings; the African History and Contemporary Black Reality classes were packed every week. However, the mission of the church required a level of humanity to which few have evolved. Even with the phenomenal, indescribable program of change co-created by the church's founder, Rev. Albert B. Cleage, who had worked with Dr. King and Malcom X, rooted in the awareness of the systemic dehumanization and "niggerization" of African American people, yet grounded in the firm belief that the Black man and woman shall rise to their former glory to lead their people, and, indeed, the world in power and righteousness, in the footsteps and example of the Black Messiah, Jesus, it was not without fault, nor was it void of egoic manipulation and exploitation. Some people just were not ready for the power and influence that came with the positions they held. Thus, it was a blessing and a curse, and it was somewhere between the two experiences that this giant found her legs to stand and realized that she was, indeed, a giant.

At a moment when she could have done the usual, went along to get along and ultimately belong, something she would have done just a few years before, she did just the opposite. At a moment when she could have found herself a good trump card to play, just to stay in the game as long as the game didn't change, she took another course. She discovered her legs and stood on them long enough to walk away, though not forever. The details of that very emotional incident are not mine to divulge though I was directly involved and affected. Suffice it to say that it was a case of the universe working in her oh so mysterious ways, her wonders to perform. She would have me stand by any means necessary and she created the necessary experience for me to do so.

I said before, nothing forces a sleeping giant to awaken like having a mouth to feed, having someone else depending on you for security, for truth, for justice, having someone else look at you with their eyes full of trust and unconditional love, wanting only that in return. The founder of the Shrine, Rev. Cleage, we called him Jaramogi (meaning Leader of the People), was often quoted as having said, "Once you awaken, you cannot go back to sleep". I'm sure Jaramogi would agree, not only can you not go back to sleep, once you stand and recognize your height, you can never sit, slump, nor slouch again, and nothing will force a giant to stand and recognize that she is, indeed a giant, like having a child to protect.

No longer in regular attendance at the Shrine, and having moved from what was called The Missionary Training Institute, a glorious phenomenon which deserves its own text, I found myself in regular attendance within my own sanctuary. I began disclosing, peeling back the layers that had grown over the power within me. Listening to that still small voice within became a religion in and of itself. Recognizing the loud mouth as the voice of ego was prerequisite for membership in the church of Norma Jo. I began reading voraciously, going inward, going inward, going inward. Did I exorcise all of my demons? No.
Did I suddenly overcome all of my fears? Unh unh. Did those feelings that had dictated, governed, and directed my life and my response to life all my life suddenly disappear? Nah, not all at once, or I wouldn't be undertaking this Life Review today. I wouldn't be Learning the Language of

Feelings today. It was part of the process, a path on the journey.

"I found God in myself. I found God in myself. I found God in myself, and I loved her fiercely."
For Colored Girls…

Mother to Daughter; It's A Matter of Principle

dedicated specifically to my daughter, Kam Enita Thomas

Looking at the path of my life, one would have to wonder. How the hell did she manage to raise a female child? Did the apple not fall too far from the tree? Was it a vicious cycle? What ever happened to the poor little eight year old who wrote the infamous note: Do you love me? Yes or No? Circle?

They say that women can't raise male children into men. Well, I've always said, "bullshit" to that. That was just more of that socio-control babble that was fed to the Black community to convince us that we were not as strong as our 400 years of surviving slavery and oppression had proven. Many good men have been raised into men by women, alone. Before the phenomenon that is dead-beat dads, there was the absent father who left home to work on the railroad and returned every month or two. There were fathers imprisoned on the chain gang for being unemployed; there were fathers who went off to make a place for their family "up North", but were never heard from again, not because they did not want to be found, but because navigating this new world was not easy. Staying free was not easy. There were countless fathers who found their destinies at the end of a rope. So, mothers reared their sons and their daughters, and they reared many a good men. My father is one.

My father had a father in the home who drowned his confused identity in whiskey and women. Papa Joe was a mulatto conceived when the Hudspeth brothers gang raped the young girl who would become my great grandmother. When he reached manhood, which, back in those days, was around the age of 14, they began taunting him about who he was. My grandmother told stories of how, even after they had married and begun their family, these father-uncles would come around on their horses and mock him. Though the man who raised him from birth, gave him his last name and tried desperately to exemplify to him what a man should be, he was a troubled individual. Given also that he wore the mulatto skin color in pre-Depression Louisiana, I concluded that it was indeed his identity that caused him so much grief. Though I cannot judge his love for her, except that he was totally unfaithful, if that says anything about his love, my grandfather, a mulatto, married a woman who was blue-black, of Haitian descent. I've often thought it was his way of rejecting anything less than Black in his eyes, but she was not enough. Still, though broken, he was a man, a father. He lived in the same home with my dad, had only one son to raise into a man; yet, it was my grandmother who bore the responsibility, and my Dad will gladly tell you that. She made him the man he became. Nearing his 90th birthday, he repeats the stories of how she taught him to hold his head up as he watched his father fall face first into his dinner plate, night after night. It was his mother, with her broken English and lack of education, who encouraged him to work alongside grown men so that he could buy long johns to wear to school under his tattered clothes in winter, and new dresses for his sisters. She taught him to save one-fourth of everything he earned. She showed him that women were to be respected when she set the date and time that she would cease to endure his father's philandering ways. Once he and his sisters were old enough to care for themselves, she planned to leave, told him, the middle child, to take care of his sisters, and how long they should wait before attempting to come and meet her. Demonstrating to him what it meant to have self-respect, determination, and resolve, she set out, walking, from Opelousas to Crowley, Louisiana seeking a new life. In my father's own words, these were the things that made him the responsible man he is today. There have been many successful African American men, from all walks of life, who have touted their mothers as the source of their success and development into responsible men, but I like my father's story best. What explains this phenomenon?

If, as sociologists and psychologists have conspired to convince the Black community, it is the father's presence that is so crucial and definitive in the development of boys, then should it not be the mother's presence that is so crucial and definitive in the development of girls ... and yes, of course, with the quality of that presence being paramount? This is not babble. As the single mother of a daughter, I have pondered this time and time again. It is worth remembering here that I entered motherhood as a young woman whose life journey was crafted on a road wrought with pot holes of alienation and rejection, of not being enough. Even in the life of my own child, I felt insignificant, of no real value to her as a mother, because I had no worth to myself. So, working hard on myself, I began to grow and develop, and I felt that because of my presence in her life, because she was priority in my life, hers was not a space she would have to share with my career goals, because she had a mother, surely she would be okay.

Are you following me? In other words, I did not anticipate daddy issues. Why would I? Boys need their dads. Okay, then, girls must need their moms. She had her mom. She was good. Right? Wrong as shit!

It's a matter of Principle. Principle is the thing. There are Principles involved, the Masculine Principle and the Feminine Principle, that have their roots in the energy system. These Principles are about energy and have nothing to do with the male and female gender assignments that were imposed upon the world in days of old. Because, however, as a society, we have been conditioned to make that connection, masculine meaning male, and feminine meaning female, I will address that manner of thinking to make my point as well.

I have come to understand that it is not the absence or presence of a person, an individual with an ego and a name that makes the difference in a child's life, but the Principle, the energy. We are, each of us, beings of duality, Masculine and Feminine, yin and yang. The heart of our life journey is balancing those energies that they ultimately merge into harmony, oneness. "Male and female created, he, them". Hmmm, interpretation is everything. One's life is negatively affected when those energies are thrown off kilter by life circumstances. It explains the phenomena that is my father and men like him who had no male person guiding and directing their lives, but became great men, as well as those men who had fathers present in their homes and lives, but still turned out to be a menace to society. Whether by divine design or the influence of a person with the necessary energy, such individuals do not experience the energy imbalance to the extent that they crave it, that it affects their being.

Once again, following the gender association embedded in our collective psyche (masculine meaning male, feminine meaning female), being attacked, rejected, denied by one's father, or the simple absence of the father results in a masculine energy imbalance sending the "victim" on a quest to create balance and harmony. The individual will typically seek to restore that masculine energy in all the wrong ways, in all the wrong places. Aggressive, violent, defensive behavior is often a quest to restore masculine energy that has been loss. Being attacked, rejected, denied by one's mother, or the simple absence of the mother figure results in a feminine energy imbalance sending the individual on a quest to restore the feminine energy and bring balance and harmony into one's life. Consequently, one searches outside one's self first. Is this 100% true in all cases? Of course not, nothing is absolute? How do I know this? I don't know; I just know that when I ask to understand what is going on in my life, sometimes I get answers.

What I did not want for my daughter, was for her to discover one day that a child support check showed up in the mail every month from a man who had opted out of his role of father, who did not want to be a part of her life. What would that teach her? Would it say to her that a man does not have to want to be with you as long as he signs the checks? Would it say that money is more important than acknowledgement, honor, respect, significance? In my 20-something year old brain, that's what I feared, and I did not want to send my little girl that message. So, I never filed for child support from my daughter's father. I had a lawyer friend once, a family friend who was trying his hand at talent management (me being one) and was concerned about my ability to pursue my dreams and adequately care for my child. He insisted that I file for support. He sent my daughter's dad a letter, but it wasn't taken seriously, and was never answered. I did not pursue it for the afore-mentioned reasons. He knew I wouldn't. I raised my daughter, hoping that his absence would not affect her self-esteem; I made sure that I said nothing negative about him that would affect how she felt about herself or him. She had a mom; she was good. Yeah, I said a couple of pages ago, that was bullshit. I just didn't know it.

At first, she seemed to have more than her share of self-esteem. By the time she was 12, I thought I was rearing a pretty strong sister. She was smart, witty, outgoing, and well-rounded. She was good at a lot of things, though dedicated to excelling at none. She was also outspoken and, unfortunately, as silly as they came, so I knew in my gut that finishing high school in public school, with the necessary school records to get into a good college, might not turn out well for her. She talked a good game, but I noticed she lacked in the follow-through department. Call it mother's intuition, if you will, but I decided to home-school her, along with a number of other students, over a 4-year period. She was afforded great experiences, had a fantastic mentor in former Houston City Council-Member and Community Activist, Ada Edwards, and enjoyed an internship at 97.9 The Box where she discovered Howard University and determined that's where she would go to college. She went off to Howard and did the typical college stuff; she passed; she failed; she won awards; she worked; she connected with people; she rebelled, etc. She was well into adulthood when I realized there was a daddy issue. Whenever I approached her about the possibility of it, even suggesting therapy, that we could go together, she would insist that she was okay.

Of course, I blamed myself. When her father decided to stick his head back into her life, after his mom died, I should never have allowed it, but I didn't think I had the right to deny her that experience. Unfortunately, it would become a pattern of sticking his head in and out. The relationship would become exactly what I feared and worked to avoid all those years. He stuck his head in, wrote a few checks, and disappeared. When she was graduating high school, I should never have included him in her Rites of Passage, but I did. In, then out. Her college graduation, in, then out. As a young adult, making unpopular decisions, needing direction, in, then out. All the while, people in our own family, within our immediate circle are praising him, speaking fondly of him, holding him up as such a great guy. As a guy, he is pretty cool; as a father, he sucks. Even I, having dealt with what I felt as his betrayal so many years before, had engaged him in my life as well. He did the music for one of my shows that my daughter performed in. I never knew she had an issue with that. Life had forced me to throw up the middle finger and keep it moving. No matter how I felt on the inside, nothing could affect my ability to push through. It was a skill I had perfected, took pride in, and presumed I had passed on to her. I never considered that she would begin to think, "If he's so great, then why does he keep rejecting me? If everybody thinks he's so wonderful, then there must be something wrong with me. Why is he so friendly and jovial and giving and patient toward others and not me? What's wrong with me?" Too much of this sounded familiar.

Again, if we adhere to the societal perception of male vs female, I would conclude that having been rejected by her father, she suffered energy loss from the Masculine Principle. Thus, her experiences in life have been about restoring that masculine energy. I have her permission to explore and express my conclusion that her defensiveness and aggressiveness are outward attempts to reclaim and restore her Masculine energy. While living, for a few months, in a house full of boys, she learned to defend herself. Rather than assertiveness, she learned aggressiveness. Hearing unflattering words said about me, not knowing who she could trust in my absence, she built a wall around herself.

[The Language of Feelings, as I have been demonstrating in this memoir, would say that divine design magnetized into her life the experience that would awaken her to her own Masculine Principle. It was life's way of saying, the Principle you seek, is already available to you; it is within you. You never have to seek outside yourself for anything.]

The failures of her relationships could very well be because guys, in the early stage of the relationship, do not initially encounter her masculine energy; it shows up later in the relationship when she is observed handling more of life's challenges on her own. They, then perceive her masculine energy assertion as a threat to their own societal conditioned view of male dominance, and it causes conflict. My poor daughter has been called many things simply because she, like her mother, has been forced to balance her energies on her own. The world can't always handle balanced energies.

I come to the end of this life review, this self-exploration, this peeling away of layers to get to the authentic core of myself having recognized that there is no layer, no aspect of myself, no position, no label, no classification, no identification, no qualification that I hold greater than that of mother. Yet, it is where I have sensed my greatest failure, where I felt most inept. I am a woman; yet, I could not build within my daughter a strong sense of self. The apple did not fall far from the tree.

I take solace, however, in the fact that herein lies my greatest opportunity to make the greatest impact on daughter's life. The most important thing I can ever share, of all that I have shared even here in this writing, is this: YOU ARE ENOUGH. You are already balanced. You possess within you both the Masculine and the Feminine Principles of the Universe. Feeling a void, you have been seeking balance, but what you seek has been within you all the time. "The kingdom of God is within you."

The absence and in-out presence of your father, and now the downright ignore-ance, was divinely orchestrated to point you in the direction of this truth. No one can give you what they do not think they possess themselves. Our best is to hope and pray that they awaken to the remembrance of it.

I conclude. Life set me up to go within myself for all those things a mother gives to a child: unconditional love, understanding, sense of self, support, safety and security, protection and defense. Absence of mother, rejection by the mother figure, even unwitting attacks on my female persona by petty girls and sharp tongued women fueled my journey. That journey compelled me to ask the big question. What is the real purpose of my existence? The answer: balancing the masculine and feminine energy, achieving balance, harmony and oneness within myself that I might project it out into the world and bring the world into that same balance, harmony, and oneness. The answer did not come that clearly worded and neatly packaged. It did not come as soon as I came upon the right question. For me, that was, and is, the definition of HOME. All of my life, I have been searching for the smell of garlic on Sunday. I have been searching for home. I have been searching for balance and harmony of my duality that they might become one, and it's not a one- time thing.

Awareness of a thing doesn't simply make it so; awareness of a thing informs the possibility of its creation.

Life set my daughter up with a set of circumstances and conditions such that the absence of her father from her life would send her in search of the Masculine Principle. She can now stop reacting to life in a manner that, like the rest of us, she, herself questions and often regrets. She can stop trying to make sense of a life that makes no sense.

"We cannot solve our problems with the same level of thinking that created them."

-Albert Einstein

My daughter can now examine every life experience that comes her way by asking: How is this experience making me feel? Do these feelings relate, in any way, to a lack of the Masculine Principle? What extenuating circumstances might be influencing what I feel as well? What is the extreme opposite of those feelings? How might I explain the Masculine Principle (energy) behind each extreme opposite? How do I get myself to that extreme opposite, into that energy?

It is important to note:
Not every fatherless child is fatherless for this reason. Not every motherless child is motherless for this purpose. Remember, this specific example is about a soul's journey, my soul, my daughter's soul. However, I'd bet it applies to a helluva whole lotta people, which is why my daughter has allowed me to share my "theory" regarding her personal journey, and why I have shared mine.

This is about evolution of consciousness, becoming more and more Spirit in a physical embodiment. My daughter and I are clearly soul-mates, here to share our like-journeys, to provide each other with the set of circumstances and conditions ripe for those journeys. Our path to transcending our physical experiences, transforming pain and disappointment into awareness and higher consciousness are definitely intertwined. It is my intent that all of the insufficiency, ineptitude, and insignificance I have felt as her mother will be waylaid by my acquired awareness as to why I had to be that person that I was in her life and in my own, at that time. It is my hope and prayer that evolution and transcendence will be far more fulfilling to her than recognition and acceptance by any individual, including her father. "Seek ye first the kingdom and all things shall be added." Balance, harmony, oneness, the kingdom, it's within you. Jesus said that; he's my brother; I believe him. I'm her mother. I hope she believes me.

EPILOGUE

it was when I stopped searching for home within others
and lifted the foundations of home within myself,
I found there were no roots more intimate
than those between a mind and a body
that have decided to be whole

                                            -rupi kaur

Comin' "Roun' the Mountain: Not Home Yet

It's a song we sang as children.
> *She'll be comin' 'roun' the mountain, when she comes. She'll be comin' 'roun' the mountain, when she comes. She'll be comin' roun' the mountain; she'll be comin' 'roun' the mountain; she'll be comin' 'roun' the mountain when she comes.*
>
> *She'll be ridin' six white horses, when she comes. She'll be ridin' six white horses, when she comes. She'll be ridin' six white horses; she'll be ridin' six white horses; she'll be ridin' six white horses, when she comes.*

Thanks to the advent of the internet, I was able to do a quick Google search and discover that the lyrics actually say, "she'll be **driving** six white horses…" Well, in my literal mind, I had already determined that this was one bad bitch to be **ridin'** six white horses all at one time, and I always wondered who **she** was. There are other verses we sang which escape my memory, some we made up, but the Google search rendered a few more about her "wearing red pajamas", "shouting hallelujah", "sleeping with Grandpa" (hmmm), and "killing a big red hen when she comes". A little Wikipedia search, Wikipedia being as extensive a search as I planned to do on this topic, revealed that it derived from a Christian song known as "When the Chariot Comes", traced back to the 17th century British Radical

Protestants, then later appeared in various ballads. By the 19th century, it had spread through Appalachia which is where the lyrics of my childhood originated. It says the song originally referred to the second coming of Christ, and the "she" was actually the chariot that the Christ would be driving. When I read that, I was prompted to take my research a little farther than Wikipedia. Then I suddenly found, among certain other sources, that the song was attributed to the Negro spirituals and was suspected to be code for the Underground Railroad.

Now, I share this little tidbit of research mainly as illustration to myself, and to those who value symbolic sight and do not believe in coincidences, who look for synchronicity in the ordinary details of life, that there is divine orchestration at work here.

I had found myself accidentally sitting in a Ministers' meeting at my church and was told by my Bishop to remain. He proceeded to instruct the Preaching Ministers to each write a sermon for which he would provide hermeneutical guidance. As he pointed to each of the Ministers, he pointed to me as well. I wanted to protest, but I didn't want to disrupt the meeting; so, I just decided within myself that I wouldn't do it and he wouldn't remember I had been accidentally present in the meeting anyway. I have delivered the message at church before, but it was for Baccalaureate Sunday, directed primarily to graduates. As Youth Facilitator, I was in charge of the program, and I did the speaking that year to avoid having to gratuitize a guest speaker. I had no intention of ever delivering a sermon again, but that one day, when the song from my childhood popped into my head, "Comin' 'Roun' the Mountain", I thought, what a good sermon title. I eventually dismissed it as a sermon and thought I would revive my blog with it, but considering I have not been able to determine who my blog audience is, or even what I really want to blog about, it sat in my binder, until now. As I neared the end of this writing experience, it came to me once again, slightly different, like an appeal from deep within me, "Come 'Roun' the Mountain".

While I am affiliated with a Christian organization, I prefer to not label or religiositize my life path. I am one who has sought to follow the example of Jesus, a brother who awakened one day to the memory of his spiritual nature as an embodiment of the Creator, discovered his inner divinity, his Christ-self, his God-self and set upon a journey to live from that Christ space and encourage others to do the same. I am who, what, and where I am today because one day I set out to discover the truth of who he was and what he was truly about.

My "religion" had begun to make less and less sense to me. I began my inquiries with, "Who is this Jesus"? When in trouble, I would ask, "So, Jesus, are you there?" When NOTHING made sense, I would say, "Look a'here, unless you want your sister to jump off into the abyss, I suggest you make some sense of all this, now, thank you." And clarity would come. Yet, over my 57 years, growing in knowledge of history and universal principle, I would return to this query numerous times, "So, who is this Jesus, again? And it is because of the answers I received, because of that relationship that grew out of the many conversations with an energy I could not see, but absolutely felt, that I continued to seek greater awareness and experience of my own divinity. Like Jesus, who says he is not, was not, and has never been the "only begotten" son of God, I believe that I, too, all of us, should be about the business of turning water into wine and moving mountains, dispelling darkness with our light, raising energy where it has been debased. So, for this reason, I embrace the Christ-I-AM path.

Now, when that little childhood ditty returned to me, which probably does have its origin in Negro spirituals and the "second coming" of the Christ, I did not perceive the mountain as an obstacle. 'Roun' the mountain symbolizes an elevated, exhalted state of being from which all of the trappings of the world which we co-created in support of our embodiments here in space and time can be seen for what they are. It defines the level of consciousness Jesus, the Christ, did achieve, that all mankind possesses but does yet embrace. It identifies that prepared place to which all mankind is expected to arrive, hence, a second coming, if you will.

Come 'roun' the mountain says to me, in the words of my big sister Kat, "Cut high, or stay at home!" Don't dwell in the valley of life; be a mountain dweller. When life is kicking your butt, come 'roun' the mountain, and from that point of view you will see that it doesn't have the power to destroy you; it has no power at all except that which you give it. From the mountain perspective you can see it for what it is; call it by name. If it's a situation you co-created, call it back! If it's a situation you have found yourself in, look and see if there is someone else who is being served by your misfortune or discomfort and either endure on behalf of your brother or sister, or choose not to; you get to choose. When the world is looking crazier and crazier by the day, "let not your heart be troubled", or "fail you for fear". Come 'roun' the mountain.

From the mountain, when you see crazy coming, you can recognize craziness as part of a bigger picture; not that you should excuse and tolerate craziness, but you will see and understand it for what it is and be able to assuage the anger, fears, worries, and concerns of others who are also willing to see from a different, a higher perspective. We can combat racism, from the mountain. We can stop police brutality, from the mountain. We can end child, spousal, and elder abuse, from the mountain. Come 'roun' the mountain!

While these writings have been about my discovery that life has been trying to point me in the direction of home, and I now recognize that as the central theme of my life, I recognize that it is not just a destination to which my soul seeks arrival one day. It is a state of being to be lived every day. My life challenge is to view every situation from this perspective. When I'm going through some go-through, the challenge is to look at how it is serving the central theme of my life, how it is requiring me to be at home, to inhale the smell of garlic on Sunday. I could ask, "What would Jesus do?" Instead, I ask, "What would I do, if I were home?" It's not easy, but I am reminded, now, to "come 'roun' the mountain". Go high. See the situation from a higher perspective. Cut high. Respond from a higher understanding of the situation. Check in with my feelings and see what they have to offer.

So, yes, I have clarified the central theme of my life … the smell of garlic on Sunday, home. I'm not there yet. I'm on my way. Every experience that comes into my life comes with the purpose of getting me there, and to get there, I must come 'roun' the mountain.

Closure

So, my step-mother, mother figure for 44 years, made her transition, January 27, 2015. I felt a grief that I did not anticipate. I think I shared somewhere in the Prologue that I had felt ashamed of myself for unintentionally causing her to feel insignificant, like an obligation to be fulfilled, then I was given the opportunity to see her for what she truly was, a soul, buried, in a death-like sleep, six feet beneath an embodiment that had experienced brokenness, a brokenness that had never been repaired or healed, not even acknowledged. The brokenness had, therefore, taken over and consumed this soul's entire experience. All that she was, or at least what she showed to the world, was a result of experiences which had left their emotional residue to shape and color her perception of herself, her world, and her relationship to it. I doubted this soul would ever awaken from this death like sleep, and remember who she was and was meant to be. So, each time I entered my parents' home from that time forward, I did not see my step-mother; I saw a soul. I saw God in that soul. I saw the breath of God inhaling and exhaling, animating, and giving life to Delores Faye Jones Robison Thomas. I know now that it was necessary that I have that experience not only for the process of closure, but Spirit knew the day would come that she would need me to render aid in a way I would never have imagined. I had to be able to provide the type of care and comfort that would be required, to show the type of love and mercy, empathy and compassion necessary.

 A little over a month before her transition, I had finished my Life Review, and had, in the process, learned the language of my feelings, and discerned what they had come to say, where they had been and would continue trying to lead me. I'm certain there could be more, or less, to that process than what I experienced, but it's what I experienced. I was able to understand why certain people had come into my life and the agreements we had made at the portal of life. My step-mother, for example, was, like my birth mother, never intended to mother me. I was never intended to experience that unconditional mother's love, a love that the word "unconditional" does no justice, a love that is unfathomable to the human mind. The love that is accepting, validating, nourishing, and all encompassing. Mine was a path that would force me to seek that love, first, in all the wrong places, ultimately finding it in the very place from which it originates, at the core and in the essence of my being, Home. Understanding, now, the role my step-mother had agreed to play, "the wicked step-mother" with ne'er a kind word to say, those once debilitating words began to fall from my memory, their sting dulled, their impact inconsequential. The course of my life, the decisions and choices I made had been very much determined by how I viewed myself, my world, and my relationship to it which were greatly due to the words that had been spoken to me. Though I had developed a mechanism for dealing with them and their source energy many, many years ago, I was now, free indeed. I neither required nor desired a tearful apology, retraction, or explanation. I knew they would never come and I did not need them to. While I must still come to terms with what feels like lost time and energy, failure and setback that could have been avoided had I perceived of myself differently than I did, had I learned to listen to my feelings aeons ago, had I not experienced this set of feelings in the first place, I understand that everything that has happened has gotten me to the me I am today, and I can live with that, on most days.

So, as we prepared for her final rites, I knew I had to stand and speak, not for her, not for anyone else in the room, though I was certain others would be helped, but for me. It would be my closure. The words were not hard to put together; so, I closed that leg of my journey saying:

> Upon deciding to speak, not just as a member of the family, but on behalf of myself and the Thomas-Jones family, I wondered for a moment how I could do that effectively since everyone who entered the Thomas household had a very different relationship with MaFaye. Then, it occurred to me almost immediately that what we do have in common is laughter. If you know my mother, really know my mother, then you know she had no filter. When she opened her mouth, whatever was inside, came out. What she said might range from the ridiculous to the sublime; what she

said might sting or rub you the wrong way, but at the end of the day, the month, or after some years, you'd probably end up just shaking your head, and laughing. I am reminded of an incident that took place one Christmas. Christmas Dinner at my parents' house has always been a big production with everybody in attendance, including our annual visit from the Jehovah's witnesses. This particular Christmas, I was in the Dining Room setting up and the doorbell rang. I could see The Watchtower booklet through the glass at the side of the door; so, I decided to hide. I think Sheky was in the room with me, and she ducked behind the piano. The doorbell rang again. MaFaye entered the foyer and saw us hiding; instantly, she knew what was going on. She threw open the door and gave a festive greeting. "Merry Christmas!" The Jehovah's Witnesses, having obviously received such greeting prior to reaching our door, ignored the salutation and went on to ask if MaFaye had time for them to witness to her and share their literature. "Oh noooooo" was her reply. MaFaye always held the word "no" for a long time. "We're getting ready to have Christmas". There was lots of music in her voice as she spoke, and a special, rising inflection at the word Christmas. Then came the clencher. "Won't you join us?!" Sheky and I could no longer contain ourselves, nor could the others in the next room who obviously heard the invitation. Who invites Jehovah's Witnesses to Christmas Dinner? Well, MaFaye did. Call it evangelism if you'd like, but I can share other instances where she just opened her mouth and let what was in there, come out, where the words from her mouth simply forced you to just laugh. As I thought of what to say here today, the song "Memories", came to me. It says …

Memories, light the corners of my mind. Misty, watercolor memories of the way we were. Scattered pictures of the smiles we left behind, smiles we gave to one another, for the way we were. Could it be that it was all so simple then, or has time rewritten every line? If we had the chance to do it all again, tell me, would we? Could we? Memories may be beautiful and yet, what's too painful to remember, we simply choose to forget. So, it's the laughter we will remember, whenever we remember, the way we were.

 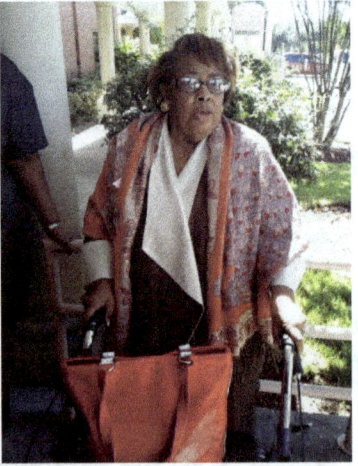

My step-mother, Delores Faye Jones Robison Thomas

1930 - 2015

Completion

The completion of the Life Review coincided with the production, *An Urban Christmas Tale*, which had come off quite well. There were about 175 people in attendance, according to the program count. The performances were great, with only one performance glitch and one technical glitch – body mics. You know, you can tell your sound people to put new batteries in the mics after sound check, but you'd better double check to see that it's done. I confess that I have yet to experience the show of my dreams, but it was a good show, well received; the audience took the journey with us and that's what matters. Plus, forty days without sugar, I even lost some weight.

Like hundreds of thousands of other people on the planet, I have talked about writing a book for a long time. I've even outlined at least two, a unique personal experience I thought was the stuff of a good book, and a series of journal entries I thought was also the stuff of a good book. I might have been right, but I followed through on neither of them. I have a few stage plays and screen plays that I've thought about converting to novels, but haven't. It was only upon taking the journey of bringing closure to my feelings about my step-mother, of single-handedly mounting a phenomenal show, and Learning the Language of Feelings in the process, did I feel a real book calling. Not only would baring my soul, cleaning all of the skeletons from my closet, and yielding to transparency take me over that last hurdle of self-awareness and acceptance, it would be an opportunity to help a lot of people, give other people courage to do the same.

I know for a fact that far too many people are walking around, feeling some kind of way, pretending it's okay, denying it, cursing themselves for complaining because "there are others who are worse off". I have come to the conclusion that no matter what caused an individual to feel a certain way about herself/himself, if that feeling is prohibiting one from being her authentic self, from behaving like a limitless soul who deserves to live like he's free, it's worth investigating.

I know for a fact that far too many people are caught up in emotional responses to situations and conditions. They are in a domino effect, unable to stop the downward spiraling momentum overtaking them, and the inciting incident is becoming their life story, a story they keep living and telling over and over again. If they could only come out of the emotion, experience the feeling, learn its language and decode the message, the lives, the lives of those around them, the world would be a much better place. That's what I did. That's what this book has been, a sharing of the documentation of that journey.

For a period of about seven weeks, I examined my feelings, feelings I had begun carrying around with me from about the age of five that had grown and deepened over the years. I called these feelings by name and looked them in the face:

Alone   Unwelcomed   Uninvited   Unaccepted
Abandoned   Motherless   Unworthy   Alienated
Inadequate   Confused   Out of Place   Forgotten
Insecure   Misunderstood   Betrayed
Different   Paradoxical

I started narrating to myself, in writing, as best as I could remember, those experiences that had left their mark on me, left me with all of those feelings that I could not seem to shake. I went back to the source of feelings I had already recognized and tried to deal with over the years, feelings that had been the topics of poems, short stories, and plays, the focus of my spirit work, even feelings I thought I had overcome, put in their perspective, or actually outgrown. I wrote them down, all of them. As best as I could, I followed each feeling back to its beginning.

I would ask, "Why did I have THIS feeling or THAT?" I kept thinking to myself that other people have had similar experiences, but were not affected in this way. After reminding me that I am not "other people", that still, soft voice I heard back in first grade, which, a lifetime later, I had learned to stop arguing with, to the extent that Listening had become my religion, would answer.

"What would you like to have felt?" The voice asked.

Of course, my response, "The opposite! I would like to have felt the opposite."

"Then go there".

So, I did. <u>I went to the extreme opposite of every feeling I explored</u>. I gave those extreme opposites names. I visualized what it would have been like had a particular experience left me with the extreme opposite of the residual emotion I felt. I asked myself how different my perceptions would have been, of myself, of my world, and my relationship to it.

Then, I wondered. I asked, where on earth, under what circumstances could I possibly find or experience those extreme opposites? In this question, I found something. I found what I call <u>Sacred Themes</u>, all hovering around and pointing to one <u>Central Life Theme</u>, the destination of the journey! Hanging out in the possibility of the extreme opposites, I suddenly understood where I had been headed the whole time. For me, it was Home, the smell of garlic on Sunday. Not a physical place, but an internal place, a state of being. I could now look at everything that happened in my life from that perspective.

So, I did, and I do. Looking at everything in my life from the perspective of the journey Home-ward, or the Central Life Theme of "home" makes all the difference in how I respond to what shows up, and how I react to it. It is the most empowered way of living I have yet to experience.

Everyone should approach life from a position of empowerment. Learning the Language of Feelings is empowering. I feel so strongly about it; I have outlined the steps I took in the pages to follow. I invite you, no, I urge you to use it and find your Sacred Themes, find the destination of your Soul's journey, your life's central theme. Make sense of your life, so you can make your life make sense.

About the Author

One would think that after a memoir, there would be nothing that hasn't already been told, but there is. There's a lot. As aforementioned, this began as a Life Review with a purpose of unearthing some deep seated, limiting beliefs that might be keeping me from fulfilling major goals and objectives in life, from fulfilling my dreams and aspirations. It turned into a journey of the Soul, Learning the Language of Feelings. That it might fulfill its purpose, take me a little higher, raise my consciousness, raise my vibration, I delved into those memories that weren't the easiest to relive. I turned the mirror on those aspects of myself that were not the prettiest to look at. Not that I feel the need to redeem myself, my journey is what it is; I am who I AM and who I AM becoming. I'd just like to tell the world a little bit more about me, let you know that I'm just like millions of others. I can do my self-work, they can too.

I am the 5th child born to Joseph and Velma Joyce Thomas; I followed Kathlynn, Pamela, Laura (who died at birth), and Mercedes. My father was born in Opelousas, Louisiana to Joseph and Josephine. My mother was born in Houston's 5th Ward to Norman and Alice Westmoreland. I can go much farther into my history via my father's lineage than I can my mother's. Perhaps, one day I will pen some words in honor of those voiceless souls. Together, my parents settled in the Acreage (Acres) Homes community, owned and operated Joe's Barber & Beauty and other enterprises, and raised their family until my mother's death.

Velma Joyce Westmoreland Thomas
1930 - 1965

Crowley, LA was my childhood home away from home. My fondest memories are of chinaberry wars, slopping the hogs at my grandma's house, and the many arguments we had at her side door because I refused to retrieve eggs from the hen house for fear of chicken snakes, or escort myself or my sister, Joby, to the outhouse after dark. I recall her warnings about going "cross dat trussa". My grandmother was Creole and broken English was her second language, but she made it very clear that we were not to cross the trestle. It was Louisiana, 1960's – early 70's, and there were some places Black people simply did not go, like through the front door of the bus station and the movie theatre, or across the trestle. I remember Ms. Monya's pear tree, another source of argument with my grandmother. My logic, anything that fell or hung over her fence into the ditch or onto the road was fair game. The aunties, Ollie Mae and Willie Mae made pancakes and sent us out to play ALL DAY, drove us past the white swimming pool to see how much fun the white kids were NOT having so that we cherished our colored pool blasting Motown sounds, and sent us up to the Youth Center to dance. They are no longer with us. Mr. Joe, Ms. Reah, Bella, Abigail, and the house filled with foster kids who ate lots of cereal for breakfast, that Youth Center that hosted dances for colored children round the way and those visiting thru the summer heat, the forbidden trussa which held uncertain tales of the KKK on the other side daring us to cross, are now all precious memories of a not so distant past. Over in Opelousas, my great grandmother, cousins that we called aunt and uncle, 2nd cousins, the Dress Man and Pumpkin Head Man, both fictitious characters meant to scare city kids to death, and the cool-cup lady who sold frozen kool-aid in a cup, all gone. Paved roads, street lights, section 8 housing have claimed our stories. Our numbers are dwindling. When we return for funerals, our conversations turn to what used to be where, who used to live where, what's wrong with Black people these days, aches, pains, and the miracles of garlic. I love who I am, where and what and who I come from, the taste of my cousin's rice that connects me to something beyond my palate....the aromas, the sounds, the sights, the textures of a culture, of a people, the descendants of those who chose to survive, to carve out a space for themselves as best they could, with me in mind, and the day I would come to carry us on. It's for all of us who chose to embody in this time that I live and carry on. It's why I do what I do, and have come to understand why I have done what I've done by default, on purpose, through insanity, and despite uncertainty.

Center-My grandmother, Josephine Charles Thomas Bourgeois; L to R: My aunts, Ollie Mae Winbush & Willie Mae Mitchell, and my dad, Joseph Thomas, Jr. They called him Tayti.

I started this journey, unknowingly, a decade out of the University of Houston, degreed in Theatre and English Education, enjoying a dual career as Performing Artist & Arts Educator. I had my Screen Actors Guild card in hand and my sights on the bright lights of Hollywood, but at some point, I determined that the Hollywood climate just might not be supportive of a young mother such as me, still coming into her own. Already sick and tired of the questions like, why don't you go audition for this super famous person, or that uber successful t.v. show, like it was really that simple, and I could but for some reason I hadn't, and, honestly, deathly afraid of failure, I told myself I'd better go the independent route to have the career I desired. So, I decided that I would write the plays and produce the films worthy of my talent, that depicted Black women as I knew them, not as Hollywood perceived them. I determined that I would nurture, develop, and train young talent to do the same, and utilize the Arts as a tool of outreach and exposure to my community.

So, upon completing a stint in Youngstown, Ohio with the productions, *Ain't Misbehavin'* and *Split Second*, and after a brief sojourn in Chicago, with my 8 year old daughter, Kam, in tow, I returned to my native Houston. While teaching in public school, I began a self-designed study of film, and developed SumAct, a summer theatre youth program which, for 5 years, provided training in the performing arts, offered enrichment in Reading and Writing, employed college theatre majors, and brought Arts to the community. Each year the summer program ended with full stage musical productions like *Nokie*, my own Caribbean adaptation of the Pinnochio story. Out of SumAct grew the Speech Choir of Houston, a tour group of young performers.

Scape Productions was designed to foster the mission of providing underserved communities with the Arts year 'round, with projects like Inter-Generational Theatre, bringing children and elders together. My original production, "Yellock's Diner", was featured at the Texas Conference on Aging. I took theatre into youth conferences, women's conferences, and worked also with programs like the Fifth Ward Enrichment Program, using theatre and creative writing with teenage fathers.

Recognizing that Kam would not get into a good college at the rate she was going, ticking teachers off, keeping up commotion, good a lot of things, committed to nothing, I decided she should be home-schooled. I was also pretty distraught with the public school system as a classroom teacher. My partner, Angela F. CeZar, and I founded Scape Africentric Umbrella Home School, enrolling sixty plus students over four years, and introducing the methodology now called Arts Integrated Instruction, to the Houston scene. Scape students were featured regularly on the radio show, Dialogue w/ Ada Edwards.

Encouraged by the notoriety my work was gaining through SCAPE and Scape Productions, as well as Theatre and Film Festivals, I founded French Creole Productions, a stage and film production company. Through FCP, came "Church Ladies", which opened at Houston's Zilkah Theatre, "Wizard of Swag", "Urban Christmas", and more. My short film "Harvest Moon", screened at the Shrine Cultural Center. Under the banner of FCP, I scripted, directed, and produced PSA's, music videos, and more.

I helped establish the M.C. Williams Alumni Association and the Black Theatre Educator's Caucus. I am a member of the Texas Educational Theatre Association, and the Texas Theatre Adjudicators' and Officials Organization. I reside in Houston, Texas with Mayasa (Angela), my partner of 25years, my daughter, Kam, who is presently completing her doctorate in Educational Leadership, and my two beautiful grandchildren, Kamiliyah and Leelah.

Learning the Language of Feelings

feeling your way to the life you desire and deserve in 7 steps

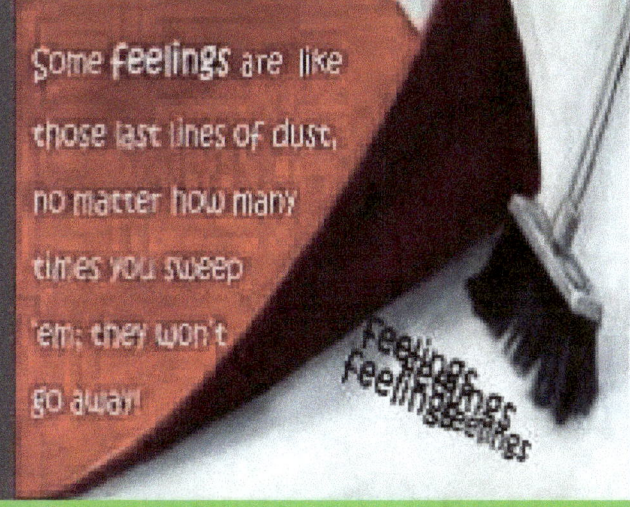

Instruction Manual

companion to

<u>The Smell of Garlic on Sunday</u>

by

Norma J. Thomas

Learning the Language of Feelings

*feeling your way to the life
you desire and deserve
in 7 steps*

INSTRUCTION MANUAL

companion to

The Smell of Garlic on Sunday
a memoir

by
Norma J. Thomas

Copyright © 2016, Norma J. Thomas
<u>Instructional Manual:</u>
<u>Learning the Language of Feelings</u>
All rights reserved.
This book, or parts thereof, may not be reproduced in any form, written, electronic, live, nor adapted without written permission from holder of copyright.
Published 2016 by: Norma Thomas
Houston, TX
Printed in the United States of America

for all of us who dare to do the dirty work,

to feel

Table of Contents

Call to Action

Count Yourself In!

Feelings vs Emotions: Feel the Difference

Types of Feelings

Getting Started

The Process

Get Clear

Get Into Your Feelings

Get To the Source

Get Past the Emotions

Get to the Other Side

Get the Message

Get Moving

E.F.F.E.C.T.

An abbreviated process for parents, guardians, and teachers of children & teens.

CALL TO ACTION

Count Yourself In!

excerpt from <u>The Smell of Garlic on Sunday</u>

In this society, if our experiences aren't BREAKING NEWS, fodder for a TMZ expose', Facebook tea, Twitter gossip, or inspiration for a new hash tag, they are nothing. Yet, the average person walking around today has had experiences that have greatly impacted his personal life, leaving behind feelings he or she has never examined, never considered as the source of all the discord, issues, and challenges plaguing his daily existence. Few realize that understanding those feelings could change the total trajectory of their lives. I like to say that if we can make sense of our lives, we can make our lives make sense. Depression is claiming so many; imagine how many could be saved if they just knew that the answer is not to rid themselves of what they feel, but explore those feelings, go into them, get into them. Instead, we are told that our issues are nothing. If they are not earth shattering we are told to suck it up or let it go. So, we don't get to feel through our experiences, and we miss out on what they have come to tell us.

Children cry, and we say, "Stop crying, or I'll give you something to cry about" – as if what he or she is crying about isn't already enough. So, they stop crying. They are no longer sad (emotion), but who knows what residue (feeling) this experience has left behind. Children get angry and pout, and we say, "Fix your face." So, they fix their faces, then what? It doesn't change how they feel; it probably exacerbates it. What if we could teach children when they are young to ask themselves: "What do I feel? What has caused me to feel this way? How would I rather feel? So, what is this feeling telling me? Now what should I do with this information?" What if we could teach them that no experience is wasted, nor the feelings left behind? What if every adult could do that for herself/himself?

Looking my dreams in the face, knowing they were right within reach, refusing to come up empty handed, I became fully aware that everything I had done in my life could all end up for naught. A lot of compromises had already been made; I had often felt like a prisoner in a prison of my own creation, attracting, meditating, vibrating by default, knowing full well that the essence, the fullness of who I AM was just within my grasp. I decided it was time to figure out what was really going on here. The common denominator I found were the feelings I held about myself, and I had the good sense to know it was time to explore what I was feeling inside.

Learning the language of feelings,
… my sanity depended on it.
… moving forward in my life required it.
… answering my life question demanded it.
… my Spirit compelled it.
… embracing who I AM prerequisite it.

The more I discounted my feelings, the more I accused my

own self of being overly dramatic, saying to myself, "Girl, that ain't nothin', least you're alive, healthy, got a job; be thankful", the more those feelings wreaked havoc in my life. I decided I wanted to make my life make sense.

At a deeper level, in what I call the Soul Space, I knew there was something that my Soul had come here to be and do and have and say, etc., etc., etc. I believed that getting to the core of those deeply held feelings would shed light on that as well, and connect me with who I AM. My life was calling me to action. I had to answer. My life mattered.

I ultimately decided that I was worth the time and energy. In the words of Miss Celie in *The Color Purple*,

> "I'm poor, black; I may even be ugly.
> But dear God! I'm here! I'm here!"

Feelings vs Emotions: Feel the Difference

What I am talking about is beyond emotion. The internet is chock full of writings on the difference between feeling and emotion, but the best explanation I can give is that feelings are what come after the emotion. Feelings are emotional residue. While emotion, the impulsive, conditioned, personal, egoic response to an incident or situation will pass, the feeling one is left with, the residual effect, takes up residence in the psyche. Think of an impactful experience in life as a high tide. The tide rolls in. The image of it might be awe-inspiring, or it might be frightful and foreboding. It elicits an emotional response. Then it rolls back out again, and the awesomeness of this vision of rising water is over, done, a memory. The fear awakened by this vision of rising water with the power to create and destroy is over, done, a memory. What remains is what the tide has washed ashore and left behind. It remains; it becomes an eyesore, a blight; it poses a danger to all in its path; it must be dealt with, or it initiates a domino effect of decay and destruction.

Emotions are fluid, malleable. They can be turned on and off, like a light switch, dependent upon conditions. Some call e-motion, energy in motion, constantly moving and changing. They come. They go. Feelings settle in.
Dr. Antonio Damasio, neuroscientist and professor at University of Southern California explains it this way, and I like it.

Emotions play out in the theater of the body.
Feelings play out in the theater of the mind.

In the text, I share this funny story to illustrate:

We were in Branson, Missouri at the Silver Dollar City amusement park. My oldest granddaughter, 4 years old, was sobbing crocodile tears because she would not be able to get onto the next ride with the love her life, her eight year old cousin, Taishyn. My heart went out to her because she had been such a trooper that day, trying any and everything the big kids tried. She was fearless! To distract her from her sorrow, I called out, "Kamiliyah! Can Bibi get a picture of her big girl?" In an instant, the crying stopped and Kamiliyah struck a pose. The great despair and heartbreak were gone, just like that. As we all turned into the next little eatery to get lemonade, her tears dried in the Missouri heat, and the outburst of emotions passed on to emotion heaven, or where ever it is they can go so quickly. Emotions linger only when we choose to hold on to them; it is in their nature to move on; they are energy in motion.

Emotions flee, but they leave their mark behind, and we call them feelings.

I'd like to believe that when we tell people to, "get over it", "leave that in the past", "let it go", or "put some dirt on it" as I often tell my grandchildren, that what we are actually telling them to do is to acknowledge and experience the emotion, then turn attention to any feelings that follow.

I hear you.

So, what do we do with our emotions?!

When a situation or event sends a jolt of energy into your body, energy in motion, e-motion, it is natural to immediately react. However, there is a rush of adrenalin caused by that jolt of energy that offers the opportunity to determine HOW one will react. That rush of adrenalin is the light switch. It comes on, and unless you are AN ANIMAL THAT OPERATES ONLY ON INSTINCT or A CHILD THAT HAS NOT GAINED EMOTIONAL MATURITY, you stop and decide whether to leave the switch on and react, physically (which includes verbally), or shut it off.

A mature, responsible, self-actualizing individual does not want that first response to propel him/her into an action that will be regretted later on. Such an individual understands the consequences of allowing emotional response to send words spewing from the mouth that can't be taken back, especially when it comes to the emotional responses that are not positive. Such an individual recognizes that rush of adrenalin as an opportunity to direct the course of history. BE ENCOURAGED: In life threatening situations, there is an inner intelligence that transcends any quick thinking we could ever employ. Oft times this intelligence compels us to react in a way we never thought we could have. In fact, Learning the Language of Feelings will most likely open the door to that inner intelligence that it might become our source, our go-to of right action.

So, what do we do with our emotions, *E*(energy) in motion? How do we keep the energy in motion from taking control?

BACK UP!

Seriously, when emotions show up, back up. Emotion is *E*(energy) in motion. What comes before *E*? A, B, C, D. Corny, but true. Watch.

- A: ACKNOWLEDGE that you are angry, afraid, sad, disappointed, hurt, pissed, whatever the emotion might be. Avoid saying "I AM (the emotion)". Say, "My emotional response to this experience is ___."

- B: BREATHE & BE STILL; decide if the situation is worthy of a response RIGHT NOW.

- C: CONSIDER the CONSQUENCES; weigh the pros

and cons of each possible responsive option that presents itself to you; ask yourself what will be gained.

- D: DO YOU w/a DISCLAIMER; Disclaimer: the YOU you present to the world is not the true YOU. The YOU you present to the world feels that everybody else is a potential threat and is, thus, ALWAYS on the defensive. So, you must decide which YOU it would be most responsible to give the power to in this situation. Which YOU do you want to represent you? Have you heard the Native American analogy of the two wolves we each have inside of us? Determining which YOU to give your power to, is like determining which wolf you are going to feed?

[You'll see this again at Step 4!]

In other words, be sure you will be able to look yourself in the bathroom mirror, or the police officer in the rear view mirror, and take ownership of your words and deeds. Emotions wreak a lot of external havoc when not harnessed immediately. The first thing a mature, responsible individual, who's trying to anchor his life to the highest expression of himself wants to do, is keep a situation from getting out of control, bring clarity to it, remain centered, reserve energy for what is most important in life, and get to what matters.

Types of Feelings

To date, I have identified two types of feelings. As time goes on and I continue to work with the language of my own feelings and help others explore theirs, I might discover other classifications of feelings, or you, reader, might recognize feelings of another kind. If so, please feel free to share in the Language of Feelings Community. Otherwise, the two I have been working with are:

1
Gut Feelings/Intuition/6th Sense

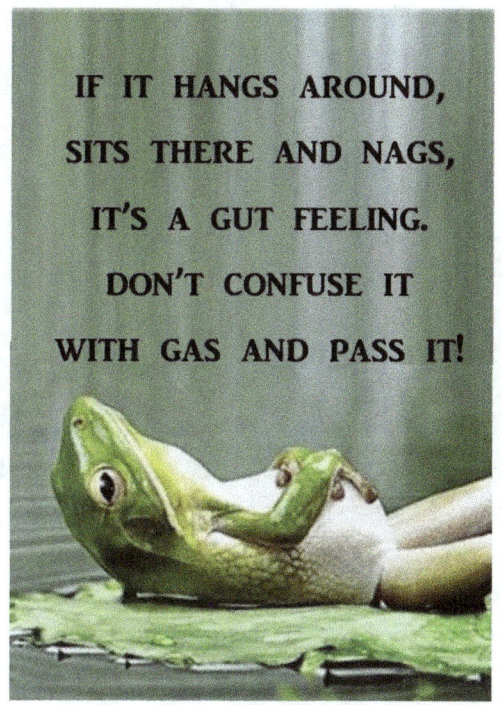

You know when somebody is lying their cane off. Don't you? You know when something is just not right. You know it's not a good situation to be in. Hmm, you feel like there's more to that story. You need to turn right here. You'd better not go that way. You don't' know how you know! You just feel it!

We often say, "SOMETHING TOLD ME not to get on that plane. SOMETHING TOLD ME not to give them my information." That something is, very often, a gut feeling, intuition, or 6th sense. It's very often that still soft voice, those spirit guides looking out for you, but equally as often, it's just a feeling. I love these feelings. It makes me feel like I'm in touch with something greater than my physical self, like a piece of wisdom or knowledge that the universe possesses is being shared with me.

> "NEVER IGNORE A GUT FEELING, BUT NEVER BELIEVE THAT IT'S ENOUGH."
>
> ROBERT HELLER

2
Emotional Residue

The type of feelings that Learning the Language of Feelings works with is the emotional residue that takes residence in our psyche. In the process of Learning the Language of Feelings, we sometimes depend upon gut feelings, intuition, and 6th sense to get to the heart of a matter, and to decipher or decode our messages, but the feelings which serve as our spiritual messengers are the residue of emotion.

Even when we responsibly address our emotions and save ourselves from ourselves, there is still the likelihood that emotional residue will remain with us, especially if it was a traumatic or impactful experience, and most especially if the experience was perceived as "negative". This residue does not compel us to act without thought, impulsively. This residue instigates thought, and typically not good thoughts; it colors those thoughts with impressions, points of view, and conclusions. This residue nurses our responses over time to the extent that it dictates how we respond to life, long term, not just in the moment.

While emotional reactions can be thwarted so that they do not create chaos, feelings are not that easily persuaded. They have come with a message and will not leave until the message is received.

SIDE BAR-
On another level, feelings are instruments of the Spirit, the inner Divinity, the I AM presence, the God Within, for communication with the Soul – the true, authentic YOU, ME, US.

> **Feelings are the broadcast system of the higher self.**

SIDE BAR TO THE SIDE BAR –
You do not have to agree with my perception of who I am in relation to the source of my existence in order to Learn the Language of Feelings; so, don't get stuck on religious or spiritual verbiage.

If you're not inclined to Spiritual contemplation, skip the SIDE BAR, but I would be remiss if I did not share that aspect of the journey which took me within myself, to my point of connection with something higher than myself in which I live, move, and have my total being. This awareness that feelings are a tool of communication took my journey farther and deeper within myself than I expected it to go when I first began the process, and I believe it made all the difference. Kind of like "the road not taken"; so, I am compelled to share it here.

BACK TO THE SIDE BAR:
What looks to us like chaos, pain, suffering, and setback, to Spirit, are just alarms triggering our remembrance of who

we are and the power we have within us, and it is not a one-time event. We are spiritual beings having a human experience; we are spirit, the very stuff of God/the Universe/the Source - individualized and incarnated into embodied Souls. For me, the story of Jesus wasn't a totally outrageous premise plausible by blind faith alone. In its unbastardized, unadulterated form and understanding, it illustrates that these physical bodies and personas we present to the world are but vessels or vehicles by which our divine selves sojourn here, adventuring through space and time. We are bound neither to them nor by them; we can transcend them. When we do, we get to glimpse life through our spiritual eyes, and what was first perceived as tragic and earth-shattering, is viewed as an opportunity to demonstrate the unlimited, unbounded possibilities of the embodied Soul. We discover that within us is the power to change all outer circumstances. Thus, effects of emotional residue on our lives might be uncomfortable, stagnating, and confusing, sometimes debilitating even, but they have remained with us because they have a message to deliver.

END OF SIDE BAR

> **So, what happens if the message is not delivered, decoded, and applied?**

Short answer, havoc. Feelings whose messages are not delivered, neither decoded, nor applied wreak havoc. As has been and will be repeated, the feelings I am speaking of impact one's perception of one's self, one's place in the world and relationship to it, typically creating mis-perceptions. One begins to live life under the influence of these mis-perceptions; so, life doesn't make sense. We keep repeating the same experiences. We keep doing the same things expecting different results, which is the definition of insanity. We keep having the treadmill experience of getting nowhere fast. We keep getting the half of, or the opposite of what we truly desire in our lives. Feelings are vibrational, and with misperceptions attached to them, we end up sending the wrong signals to the Universe, to God, to the Source of all Things, to the Great Spirit, etc., etc., etc.

Getting Started

<u>The Smell of Garlic on Sunday</u> chronicled one soul's process of getting into her feelings, learning the language of those feelings, decoding their message, applying that message to every facet of her life from that moment forward, and *feeling her way to the life she desired and deserved.*

The learning process was a six-week journey that was well worth the time and energy. You may choose to work through this process every day for a specific period of time each day, until you are done, or once per week, on a specific day, at a specific time until you are done. Look at your calendar and decide which days and times will work best for you. Don't leave it to chance; commit for the long haul.

> **BEFORE YOU START**
> **Set a schedule you can commit to.**

- Find a partner or small group to work with ONLY if you feel you need others to help keep you on task. If you choose this route, be sure you are with others you trust with your openness and vulnerability.

    If working in a small group setting, make it a rule,

RULE: NO FEEDBACK WHEN SHARING JUST LISTEN

- Find a quiet, comfy space that will become your regular spot.
- Find a few pieces of inspirational music that you can alternate throughout the process.
- Keep your Feelings Journal on hand to record your answers, notes to self, awarenesses, and ah ha's. Save the Manual for future use; you will need to do this again next year. It is recommended that once you learn the language of those deep seated feelings that have been with you for awhile, go through the process regularly to work through new experiences, and at least once/year to address those feelings that sneaked in while you were busy with life. Soon, you will become adept at addressing them as soon as they show up.
- Breathe!
- Don't Judge Yourself!
- Go With the Flow!

SE7EN

Steps to a LIFE that makes Sense, the Life YOU Desire & DESER7E!

*

*To get where you want to go,
you gotta get going.*

STEP 1: GET CLEAR

Complete the following statement.

> At this point in my life, it is necessary for me to undertake this journey because _____.

SAMPLE ANSWER
At this point in my life, it is necessary for me to undertake this journey because I have spent so many years and worked so hard, sacrificing so much to achieve my goals, fulfill my dreams, and live on purpose, but I feel I have only scratched the surface of my potential. Either something is standing in my way, like fear, limiting beliefs, or I am on the wrong path. Though these are things I love to do, have the gifts, talents, and skills to achieve, it's just not happening. I need to get to the core of what's going on in my life.

> **AT EVERY STEP**
>
> **GET CLEAR!**
>
> **REMEMBER WHY YOU ARE DOING THIS AND WHY IT MATTERS TO YOU**

Feelings are the broadcast system of the higher self.

STEP 2: GET INTO YOUR FEELINGS

What personal feelings have you experienced over the years or recently, that seem to define you, or make you feel a certain way about yourself? Think about strong feelings you feel or have felt that seem to impact how you view your relationship to others and the world around you. Especially, identify those that make you uncomfortable, that feel a little negative, that stir up something deep inside of you, which do not reflect what you desire to feel about yourself. Make a list or let it flow:

SAMPLE ANSWER A

With regards to how I have perceived myself and my relationship to the world around me, I have always or often felt:

Alone	Unwelcomed
Betrayed	Inadequate
Uninvited	Motherless
Different	Unaccepted
Alienated	Misunderstood
Insecure	Forgotten
Unworthy	Out of Place
Abandoned	

SAMPLE ANSWER B

With regards to how I perceive myself and my relationship to the world around me, most recently, I have begun to feel misunderstood. I feel like things I say are taken the wrong way, or people have developed opinions about me that have nothing to do with who I really am. Right now, I feel like I am going out of my way to be accepted, to be part of the group. I also feel trapped, like I am doing things I really don't want to do because it is expected; it is tradition; or, it's what I've been taught. While I used to feel inadequate, that no longer plagues me, but it affected a great part of my life and caused me to make decisions I might not have made.

Don't shoot the messenger.

STEP 3: GET TO THE SOURCE

A. Look back over the feelings you listed in Step 2. Think back to when you might have first experienced each feeling. Most likely, it is the emotional residue from an impactful, emotionally charged experience. Relate the details of each experience as best you can remember it. We'll call these experiences, Inciting Incidents.

SAMPLE ANSWER

FEELINGS	INCITING INCIDENTS
Alone Forgotten Betrayed Inadequate	Kindergarten - there was a party going on, but I sat alone, not mingling or playing with the other kids. They seemed to be having so much fun. My memory is that I wanted to play, but for some reason, I did not. I think I wondered, if they would play with me. 1st Grade – I was placed in a class with students who did not perform well in school. There were others who were on grade level, but I felt like I was in a "retarded" class and nobody cared, nobody took the time to see that I was not "retarded". I could see the "smart" kids in Mrs. Treadville's class from the coat rack.

GET TO THE SOURCE Cont....

Misunderstood Judged Abused	By Middle School, I didn't have friends. I was actually pretty shy and felt inadequate compared to the other girls; yet, they called me stuck up. At church, I had friends; we were close, but I always felt certain adults judged and condemned me more harshly than they did others. I always felt like I was on guard. As silly as we were, I never felt like I could just let loose like the others. My stepmother never said anything positive to me. There were always comments putting me down, comparing me to my step-sister. She didn't do it just to me, but I felt it.
Trapped	About six months ago, I started feeling trapped. I agreed to do some things that I realized I didn't want to do. I felt obligated to do them, like I couldn't change my mind. Whenever I inquired as to whether there was someone else who could do them, I was ridiculed and browbeaten. There have been other situations too, like …

*Emotions make us human.
Denying them makes us beasts*
                              - Victoria Klein

STEP 4: GET PAST THE EMOTIONS

Review Step 3. Go back and add the emotional charge, the emotional response and/or physical reaction that resulted from each inciting incident, as best you can. Acknowledge the emotion; you might have to go back and be that person you were then, experience that pain, anger, sadness again. So very often, we are forced to keep it moving. There's no time to stop and deal with the situation. Something or somebody else is more important than we are right now; so, we cannot attend to our emotions. We are told to "put your big girl panties on". Then there are those times when we are forced to react immediately, and we react so immediately, we never get to the emotion behind the reaction. We react to protect others; we react as a show of force; we react because it's simply the straw that broke the camel's back. This is an opportunity to acknowledge that there was an incident and that incident affected you emotionally. You matter enough to stop and take a look.

WARNING
Get In; Get Out

You're not settling in for the winter. Get in your emotions and get out. Emotions are low vibrational. We all learned about energy in High School Physics class. Everything is energy; energy can neither be created nor destroyed, only transferred; energy is light vibrating at varied frequencies. Matter is a result of energy vibrating at its lowest possible frequency. Think of a light bulb, 10 or 15 wattage, placed in a lamp at the center of your den or family room. Even with no lamp shade, there's not much illumination in the room. You can't read by that light; you can't search for the t.v. remote in that light. It's virtually of no use. There's not a lot you can do with low vibrational energy either. Whatever you manage to create with it, will not last; the physical manifestation of low level energy will disintegrate into nothingness and the energy will remain as stagnant as it was before you attempted to create with it. So, the idea is to acknowledge your emotions, then get out of them.

If you choose not to get out, you, now, are the perpetrator, the harbinger of ill-will into your life, your own worst enemy. Hanging on to emotions is like picking at the scab of a sore that time and conditions have created so that healing might begin underneath. If you choose to hang on to the emotions you examine here, you will negate all of the work you have done to avoid repeating that same incident again. Remember, you said to yourself. "I'll never do that again". If you choose to hang on to the emotions, you will drag yourself down into the lowest vibration of energy in your personal field. That's when crazy stuff starts happening and we don't understand why. That's when life ceases to make sense, and everything we touch seems to turn to dust and we blame it on the devil. Remember, low vibrational energy as the source of any physical creation cannot sustain what has been created; it will not last. There is a song that says, "Only what you do for Christ will last." I have in recent years thought to myself. Perhaps, the lyricist should have said, "Only what you do THROUGH the Christ will last". Only what you do through the use of the highest vibrational energy frequency available to you, will last.

In the feelings, in the residue these emotions have left behind, is where you want to hang out for a minute, but just a minute. Even in examining your feelings, the objective is to find out what they've come to say to you. Decode the language, decipher the message, then get out. Don't double dip or go back for seconds. Let it go. In fact, letting go will be a very natural part of the process. It might not happen immediately, as soon as you have qualified the message, but it will go and you must let it.

If you find yourself replaying the **incidents** and not fulfilling the objective for recalling them to memory, or if you find yourself hanging on to the **emotions** that left you **feeling** some kind of way, rather than, getting in and out and on to the next step, then you might want to ask yourself a few questions. "What am I getting from it?" Be honest in your answer. Ask. "Does reliving this experience keep me in the position of victim and the perpetrator in the position of villain? Is this my assurance of justice"? Perhaps, it brings you attention from others, keeps you and your issues at the center of conversation. Does it give you an excuse for not taking responsibility for the forward movement of your life? Whatever the answer, whatever you are getting out of rehashing the experience, holding on to the emotions, and staying in those feelings, I offer to you here and now, this final warning. Get in; get out.

A. ACKNOWLEDGE THE EMOTIONS

SAMPLE ANSWER

FEELINGS	INCITING INCIDENTS	EMOTIONAL RESPONSES & REACTIONS
Alone Forgotten Betrayed Inadequate	Kindergarten party 1st Grade class	Sadness Withdrew more Anger Fear Set out to prove I was "smart"
Misunderstood Alienated Different Judged	Girls at school People at church	Despair Frustration Tried to fit in Rebelled Acted out Stopped caring
Trapped Oppressed	Couldn't change my mind about a commitment	Anger Guilt Screened calls

If you are emotionally charged by a recent incident or a right now incident, remember:

BACK UP!

Seriously, when emotions show up, back up.
Emotion is *E*(energy) in motion. What comes before E?
A, B, C, D. Corny, but true. Watch.

- A: ACKNOWLEDGE that you are angry, afraid, sad, disappointed, hurt, pissed, whatever the emotion might be. Avoid saying "I AM (the emotion)". Say, "My emotional response to this experience is ___."

- B: BREATHE & BE STILL; decide if the situation is worthy of a response RIGHT NOW.

- C: CONSIDER the CONSQUENCES; weigh the pros and cons of each possible responsive option that presents itself to you; ask yourself what will be gained.

- D: DO YOU w/a DISCLAIMER; Disclaimer: the YOU you present to the world is not the true YOU. The YOU you present to the world feels that everybody else is a potential threat and is, thus, ALWAYS on the defensive. So, you must decide which YOU it would be most responsible to give the power to in this situation. Which YOU do you want to represent you? Have you heard the Native American analogy of the two wolves we each have inside of us? Determining which YOU to give your power to, is like determining which wolf you are going to feed?

B. EXTRACT THE EMOTIONS

Remember, this is not about excusing the perpetrator or the instigator of the incident, or lessening the impact it has had on your life. This is about liberating you from the effects of it. Extracting the emotion is pulling the emotional attachment from the incident, pulling you out of it so that you can step back and take an objective look at it. In a few minutes, you are going to be asked to employ a little symbolic sight, to look at things symbolically. That cannot happen as long as emotions that have neither been acknowledged nor dealt with linger. Old folks used to say, "Speak of the devil and he will appear. Call him devil to his face and he must flee." Sounds good. Equate that old devil to the low vibrational energy of emotions and it makes a good point.

One of the best ways to extract emotion from a situation, experience, or incident is to view the experience differently. Look at it from a different point of view. Change your perspective, and there is always another perspective, especially after the fact. After the fact, an array of variables that are not as obvious in the heat of the moment suddenly appear. So, go back. Review the incident. Acknowledge the emotional charge that resulted. Allow a new set of variables to be applied. See the incident from a new perspective. Extract the emotion.

Ask yourself:

1. What extenuating circumstances, beyond the inciting incident itself, might have caused the emotional charge and contributed to my emotional response? Sometimes, things cannot be avoided; no one person is to blame; the situation isn't even about you, but you don't realize it at the time; age has played a factor in perception; someone is being forced by another to do or say; etc.

2. Did any good come from the experience? Did I learn something about myself, about life, about my relationship with others involved? What was gained?

> **Change Your Point of View**

SAMPLE ANSWER

EMOTIONAL RESPONSES REACTIONS	EXTENUATING CIRCUMSTANCES	LESSONS & GAINS
Sadness Withdrew more Anger Set out to prove I was "smart"	I was a very literal child. I was a little shy; in fact, I was a classic child introvert, but did not have that language or self-awareness as the time. I thought I was weird. They were kids; I was a kid. There was an element of classism in the Black community that I wasn't aware of.	I really was different. By withdrawing, I missed out on group think, became an independent thinker. I proved to myself what I could do.
Frustration Tried to fit in Rebelled Acted out Became sneaky	Because I proved I was smart, people had higher expectations for me. No mother thinks anyone is good enough for her son. Teen girls are cliquish.	You never see yourself the way others do. I realized early that I had issues.

Extract the Emotions Cont…

EMOTIONAL RESPONSES REACTIONS	EXTENUATING CIRCUMSTANCES	LESSONS & GAINS
Anger Guilt Screened calls	The people who requested my services really felt there was no one else who would do it the way that I would, but that does not excuse their inability to accept that I could no longer accommodate them or the project.	Take time before committing. I can say "no". People will push as far as you allow.

The knowing of one thing is contingent upon the knowledge of its opposite. You cannot perceive of an up if you have never been down.

STEP 5: GET TO THE OTHER SIDE

Using the information gathered in Steps 2 and 3, ask yourself what you would have "preferred" to feel, as a result of each incident. It is highly probable that you would have preferred to feel the "extreme opposite" of what you felt. Identify the **EXTREME OPPOSITE** of each feeling.

SAMPLE ANSWER

FEELINGS	FEELINGS OF EXTREME OPPOSITE
Alone	Embraced
Forgotten	Befriended
Betrayed	Connected
Inadequate	Considered
	Defended
	Enough
	Limitless
Misunderstood	Considered
Alienated	Accepted
Different	Included
Judged	Celebrated
	Absolved
	Liberated
Trapped	Respected & Honored
Oppressed	Compassion
	Regarded

"You cannot connect dots looking forward; connecting dots requires you look behind."
— Steve Jobs

STEP 6: GET CONNECTED

Spend a little time with the Extreme Opposites. Consider…

| If I hadn't felt … | → | I would never have desired to feel… |

Deep seated feelings have come into your life and affected how you perceived yourself, your place in the world, and your relationship to it, and most often in a "negative" way. Yet, when examined, these feelings point you to where you belong, what you desire and deserve in life, who you truly are. Our human eyes lie to us; so, we must practice looking behind, beyond, or in the opposite direction of what we see. When we do, we will discover the vision that life holds for us until we can see it for ourselves.

The extreme opposite of those deep seated feelings reveal what you, a divine soul, have come to experience. Life, however, has taught us to think, and feel, and see the worst, to deny our-selves what we desire and deserve in life. So, when we do admit our hopes and dreams openly, we feel guilty about it. Religion shames us into accepting less, viewing pain and suffering as punishment for sins or a badge of honor and ticket to heaven for sainthood. Our Spirits are calling us forward to the highest expressions of life.

A. For each Feeling of Extreme Opposite, describe where, in what ideal situations, and under what ideal circumstances could each desired and deserved feeling of extreme opposite have been experienced? In a perfect world, over which you had full control, what would have happened?

SAMPLE ANSWER

FEELINGS OF EXTREME OPPOSITE	IDEAL SITUATIONS & CIRCUMSTANCES
Embraced Connected Considered	Ideally, someone, an adult, would have recognized that I was alone and perhaps encouraged me to go and play with the other children, or set up a situation in which children such as I were facilitated in interacting with the other children.
Defended Enough Limitless	Someone would have recognized my capabilities and stood up for me, despite who my parents were or were not. Someone would have asked me how I felt and encouraged me to do all the things I believed I could. There would have been no racism or Black classism.
Accepted Included Celebrated	Ideally, I would have been born with or raised in an environment that new the importance of building high self-

Absolved Liberated	esteem and I would have accepted myself rather than desire to belong where I did not. That self-esteem would have kept me from doing things that degraded me, or put me in a negative light, making me feel worse about myself. With a high self-esteem I would not have sought approval of others any more than the average child/teen seeks approval of parents and authority figures.

B. Here is where that other type of Feeling comes into service, Gut Feelings/Intuition/6th Sense. For each Ideal Situation & Circumstance, find its theme. I call them "Sacred Themes" because herein lies the message(s) that your Spirit Self has encoded in your deepest feelings. These are the themes by which you can measure every deep, impactful feeling you experience in the future. From this point on, you will know what each incident, experience, situation, or circumstance and its emotional residue that comes into your life has come to tell you that you truly deserve, and what life has just for you.

Here, is also where you will employ a little symbolic sight as I mentioned in Step 4. In pairing the Sacred Theme with each ideal situation and circumstance, think of what the ideal situation and circumstance symbolize as well.

SAMPLE ANSWER

IDEAL SITUATIONS & CIRCUMSTANCES	SACRED THEMES
Ideally, someone, an adult, would have recognized that I was alone and perhaps encouraged me to go and play with the other children, or set up a situation in which children such as I were facilitated in interacting with the other children. Ideally, I would have been born with such a free spirit or an adult would have told me that it was okay to not be able to make friends easily; there was nothing wrong with me; I was okay.	Care Protection Guidance Self-Awareness Self-Power Liberation
Someone would have recognized my capabilities and stood up for me, despite who my parents were or were not. Someone would have asked me how I felt and encouraged me to do all the things I believed I could. There would have been no racism or Black classism.	Care Protection Self - Awareness Personal Power Limitlessness Oneness

Ideally, I would have been born with or raised in an environment that new the importance of building high self- esteem and I would have accepted myself rather than desire to belong where I did not. That self-esteem would have kept me from doing things that degraded me, or put me in a negative light, making me feel worse about myself. With a high self-esteem I would not have sought the approval of others any more than the average child/teen seeks approval of parents and authority figures.	Honor of Self Self-Love Liberation

C. Connect the Dots

Fill in the dots with what you have recognized, or intuited, as your Sacred Themes. What thoughts, concepts, beliefs, should inform your actions and decisions going forward? What purpose(s) should everything in your life serve? What extreme opposites of the feelings you have held should you seek in every experience? Add Sacred Theme dots as needed.

SAMPLE ANSWER

*Now that you know you're the forest,
stop being a tree.*

STEP 7: GET MOVING

You've connected the dots, identified your Sacred Themes, now get them moving in your life. As experiences arise, choose to act based on the Sacred Themes of your life. In the meantime, stay awake, stay present in your life.

Here are some things you can do:

A. Write a letter to your Former Self, the Former Self who did not know what all the experiences were for, the Former Self who endured the emotional residue. Thank your Former Self for the journey.

B. Write a letter to your Now Self. Congratulate your Now Self for taking the necessary steps to get clear about the Sacred Theme(s) of your life that you might understand the rest of the journey to come, able to address every new experience, situation, and circumstance in life from that standpoint. Thank you Now Self for acknowledging and extracting negative emotions so they have no effect on future actions or behaviors.

C. Write a Letter of Commitment to your Future Self. Affirm:

I embrace every experience that is drawn into my life either by my own unguarded thoughts or by my intended will. I work daily to discern the message of every experience, remain aware and in a state of increasing remembrance of who I am and the Divine Destination to which I am traveling.

D. Affirmations

E. Meditation – Meditation is not confined to sitting in the lotus position; walking, cleaning, sitting quietly in an ambient space are all conducive to meditation. You might even make use of some of the Guided Meditations that can be found on the internet. Be selective.

F. Inspirational readings that support your efforts and intentions

G. Join the *Smell of Garlic Community* on the web.

What about the children?

Learning the Language of Feelings

an abbreviated process for parents, guardians, and teachers of children & teens

E.F.F.E.C.T

Examining the Force of Feelings and Emotions in Children & Teens

Instruction Manual

companion to

<u>The Smell of Garlic on Sunday</u>

<u>by</u>

Norma J. Thomas

Learning the Language of Feelings

an abbreviated process for parents, guardians, and teachers of children & teens

E.F.F.E.C.T.

Objective:
Examining the Force of Feelings & Emotions in Children and Teens

Process:
- **E**MOTIONS
- **F**EELINGS
- **F**ACTS
- **E**XPECTATIONS
- **C**ONNECTIONS
- **T**AKE-AWAYS

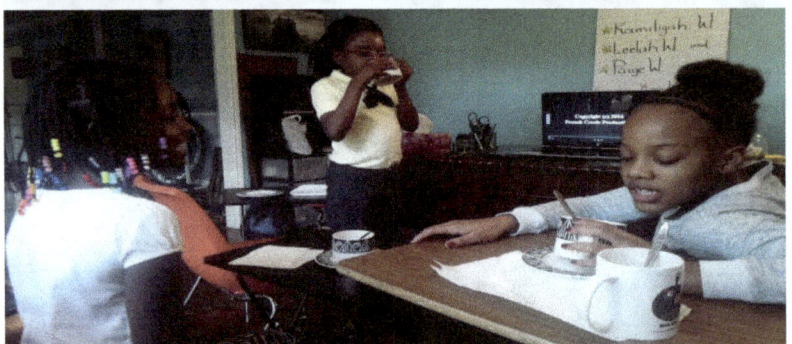

NT Conservatory, The Prodigy School
Homeschool Project

Each day began with Meditation, Yoga, Tai Chi, and Herbal Verbal. Meditation helped us become centered and focused; yoga opened us up and removed energy blocks; tai chi got our energy flowing and made us receptive to new ideas; the herbal verbal was an opportunity to express one's self on various topics, explore thoughts, emotions, and feelings, and learn that it's okay and necessary to do so.

For Parents/Guardians/Teachers

Despite, and, indeed, because of what is going on in our world today, especially this country, children should be taught that life is meant to be good. Feeling bad about one's self and others is not okay. Acting and reacting without thought and self-control is the sign of emotional immaturity. Children must be taught how to process the exterior provocations and emotional charges that show up in their lives and it is the duty of parents, guardians, teachers, mentors, and spiritual leaders to do the teaching. It is not to be left to chance or peer influence.

My eldest granddaughter, who was 10 years old at the time, overheard a family conversation about Isis. She suddenly became afraid and began to cry. She wanted to know if Isis could invade our subdivision and why people are always trying to control what other people do. We had to assure her, as best we could, that we were safe. We had to explain that there are simply people in the world who fear everything and everybody unlike themselves or believe the opposite of what they believe. We explained that when minds are closed and egos prevail, such people strike out at what they fear. We further explained that we could not let them take away our joy of living, that when masses of people stand up against intolerance of all kinds, then groups like Isis can be defeated. We assured her that people around the world are beginning to take a stand against bigotry in all of its many forms and we would do the same.
Several months later, the day before Thanksgiving, the

younger grand walked into the room with a piece of artwork. It was quite good. I asked what it was supposed to be. She said it was a group of children, dressed as "Indians", surrounding the earth.

I gasped. It seemed our annual Columbus Day and Thanksgiving Day lessons had not sunk in. After reminding her that we refer to "Indians" as Native Americans, I asked why the children were dressed that way. She said, "The children want to say thank you to the Native Americans. So, they just dressed up like them because they admire them and appreciate them." While my mind wanted to wander off into a great lesson on the difference between cultural appreciation and cultural appropriation that we, on both sides of the argument, could learn from this artwork, I inquired. "What do they want to say thank you for"?

"Thank you for protecting the earth."

I let go a sigh of relief and told her that her artwork was very creative and quite appropriate. I explained what was happening in North Dakota and showed her and the older one pictures and videos of the Dakota Access Pipe Line protests. We talked about keeping agreements, and basic human rights like access to clean water. To help them understand water contamination, I showed them pictures of the water that the people of Flint, Michigan have had to drink, cook with, and bathe in for years. The younger began to cry, and asked when we were going to move to another country. I asked why she wanted to move. We had joked about it after the Presidential election, and I was afraid she had gotten the wrong message.

She answered. "People in this country are so mean."

I told her that we would not be moving, that we would remain and do our part to stop the effects of greed and injustice. I grabbed the quote about evil prevailing when good men do nothing and shared with her all of the many ways that our household strives to do its part.

I share these little anecdotes to illustrate how our children are affected by the world they live in. They are not oblivious to what is going on around them and it does make them feel a certain way. Parents, guardians, teachers, mentors, and spiritual leaders must recognize how easy it is for our children to feel so overwhelmed and powerless that they accept injustice, oppression, crime, exploitation, terrorism in all of its forms, etc. as a way of life, as the "new normal". If they are not facilitated in processing what they see and hear, it becomes even easier for them to personalize those feelings of inadequacy, powerlessness, insecurity as who they are, how they view themselves, their immediate world, and their relationship to it.

We often wonder how good children go bad, when, in many cases, feelings left unexamined have influenced choices and decisions. Take the two seven year old boys in recent news, one white, one Black, who each took their parents' vehicle and went for a ride. The white kid, when asked why he took his parents' car said that he wanted to go on a "joy ride". He ended up on a television talk show where he was reminded, amid huge smiles and pats on the shoulder, of how dangerous a "joy ride" could be. After receiving a gift from the talk show host, he was reminded that a car is not a child's toy, "buddy". The Black kid, on the other hand, when asked why he took the car, responded that he liked doing "hood rat stuff" with his friends. This kid had not only criminalized his own behavior, but was further criminalized by the news media, and berated by neighbors and family members on the scene; social media convicted him to a lifetime of imprisonment. There was not one report of anyone sitting down with this child and asking him. "Why do you think of yourself as a 'hood rat'?"

Not only should this child's self-perception be questioned, but why did this child determine the behavior to be "hood rat stuff" while the other considered the exact same activity to be a "joy ride"? He was not born with these feelings and ideas; they were engrained from somebody's words, some type of experience. Something made him feel that he was no good and there was no one to help him decode the language of that feeling. Children and youth must be taught as early as possible to decode the message of their feelings, and apply that message to their lives. This only requires that someone cares enough to hold regular conversations, and could mean the difference between developing well-balanced, productive members of society, or individuals who become self-deprecating adults preying on others to fill their personal voids. Parents, guardians, teachers, mentors, and spiritual leaders must check in with children regularly, especially when "negative" experiences occur.

Use the acronym EFFECT:

Examining the Force of Feelings & Emotions in Children & Teens

I chose the acronym EFFECT because I remember how I wanted to be the primary influence in my daughter's life. I wanted to be her foundation, her source, the little voice in her ear until she could discern the sound of her own. I wanted my words, my example, and our experiences to have the single most powerful effect on her personal growth in a profoundly positive way. I know. It was ambitious of me. I chose it also because it's time that we as parents, guardians, teachers, mentors, and spiritual leaders, take back that power, that we impact this generation of youth in the manner in which we seem to have missed with the previous generation. Otherwise, feelings that could provide guidance in life and influence decision-making, if not understood, could impact how they view themselves, the world around them, and their relationship to it in negative ways. Teaching children to learn the language of their feelings will ensure they develop into whole, actualized human beings.

While the process of Learning the Language of Feelings, for adults, is different only in the amount of time spent and depth undertaken at each step, the acronym EFFECT is intended to even further simplify the process for young people and help them to remember the "order of operations" that they can apply at any time. When children or teens act out, are not being their usual selves, seem down and a little depressed, undergo an emotionally charged experience, especially negative emotions, guide them in examining the force of feelings and emotions within them.

Guide them through the process as often as possible, and teach them to use it on their own. Whether they are working alone are under your guidance, encourage them to write out their responses.

Learning the Language of Feelings

an abbreviated process for parents, guardians, and teachers of children & teens

E.F.F.E.C.T.

Objective:

Examining the Force of Feelings & Emotions in Children and Teens

Process:

EMOTIONS
FEELINGS
FACTS
EXPECTATIONS
CONNECTIONS
TAKE-AWAYS

Emotions

Define: a surge of energy that makes you want to take retaliatory action in response to whatever caused it.
Explain: Emotions do not last. You may be angry, frustrated, sad right now, but it will not last. Do all that you can to avoid responding to the emotional charge. First…

BACK UP!

When emotions show up, back up. Emotion is *E*(energy) in motion. What comes before *E*? A, B, C, D. Corny, but true. Watch.

- A: ACKNOWLEDGE that you are angry, afraid, sad, disappointed, hurt, pissed, whatever the emotion might be. Avoid saying "I AM (the emotion)". Say, "My emotional response to this experience is ___."

- B: BREATHE & BE STILL; decide if the situation is worthy of a response RIGHT NOW.

- C: CONSIDER the CONSQUENCES; weigh the pros and cons of each possible responsive option that presents itself to you; ask yourself what will be gained.

- D: DO YOU w/a DISCLAIMER; Disclaimer: the YOU you present to the world is not the true YOU. The YOU you present to the world feels that everybody else is a potential threat and is, thus, ALWAYS on the defensive. So, you must decide which YOU it would be most responsible to give the power to in this situation. Which YOU do you want to represent you? Have you heard the Native American analogy of the two wolves we each have inside of us? Determining which YOU to give your power to, is like determining which wolf you are going to feed?

Be sure you will be able to look yourself in the bathroom mirror, or the police officer in the rear view mirror, and take ownership of your words and deeds. Emotions wreak a lot of external havoc when not harnessed immediately. The first thing a mature, responsible individual, who's trying to anchor his life to the highest expression of himself wants to do, is keep a situation from getting out of control, bring clarity to it, remain centered, reserve energy for what is most important in life, and get to what matters.

Ask: What emotional charge did I have as a result?

If exploring a recent incident...

Ask: What emotion(s) am I experiencing right now?

FEELINGS

Define: the residue of emotion.

Explain: Once an emotion is gone or stored away in the mind/body, a feeling remains, usually accompanied by descriptive thoughts about one's self. A feeling does not typically inspire retaliatory action, but can affect how we view ourselves, our world, and our relationship to it, thereby, impacting and influencing subsequent choices and decisions. While we want to rid ourselves of emotions and feelings, we want to spend a little time with feelings before releasing them. Feelings help us understand what's going on in our lives, and contain vital information about moving our lives forward.

Ask: What feeling(s) did the emotional charge brought on by the incident being addressed leave you with?
Right now, lately, or for awhile, how would you say you have been feeling about yourself?

FACTS

Define: details of the incident *from all perspectives.*

Explain: It is important to be clear about what actually happened. Many times our emotions are charged by what we perceive, not by what actually took place. Examining the incident from all perspectives, considering extenuating circumstances that were not considered in the heat of the moment, even acknowledging the good that came out of it help to put emotions in check, and make it easier to address the feelings we have held about ourselves as a result.

Ask: What happened? Who did or said what? How? Why?

Ask: How would the other individuals involved relate the incident? How might it look from their perspective?

Ask: What emotions did you experience as a result?

Ask: Are there any extenuating circumstances?

Ask: If you were to take yourself out of the situation, become an observer, what might your thoughts about the incident be?

Ask: What was gained or learned from the experience?

EXTREMES

Define: those feelings the farthest opposite of what one now feels or has felt

Explain: To the extreme opposites, is where the feelings have come to guide you. Rarely do we desire for ourselves what we are intended to have, be, or do; when we do feel the desire to have, be, or do the seemingly impossible, we feel guilty, like we have no right, like we don't deserve it. The extreme opposite tells you where you should be and calls you to it. The extreme opposite is where your Spirit, your heart, your Soul, God, or whoever is telling you, you belong, what it's telling you, you deserve, who it's telling you, you are meant to be.

Ask: Looking back at the Feelings described earlier, what would you prefer to feel or preferred to have felt?

Ask: Looking back at the Facts, how would you have preferred the incident to play out?

CONNECTIONS

Define: elements to be used in decoding the message

Explain: Here is where you make use of a 2nd type of feeling, your gut feeling/intuition/inner guidance. The Extreme opposite of what you have been feeling represents a big picture. What does that picture look like? How would you describe it?

Ask: Looking back at the Extremes you said you would prefer to feel or preferred to have felt, what is the big picture each represents? For example, FEELING REJECTED, the EXTREMES I would prefer to feel are ACCEPTED and INCLUDED. The BIG PICTURE, bigger than acceptance and inclusion might be UNITY or ONENESS.

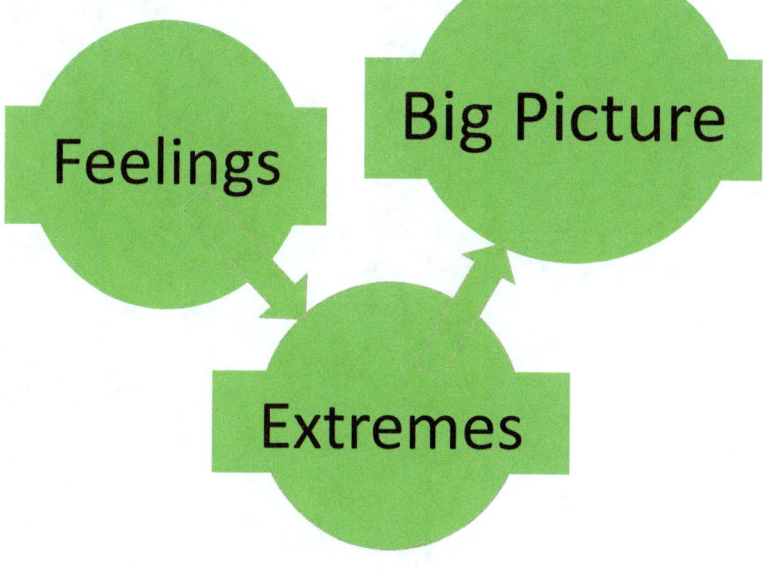

Take-aways

Define: the message, awareness, guidance received

Explain: The Big Picture is the direction you must strive for in all things. If a situation does not allow you to experience that big picture or something akin to it, it is probably not for you. You are the master of your fate and the captain of your soul. Here is where you begin to create the life you desire to live. Your feelings have led you to the big picture; you must repeatedly seek to create situations and experiences, or find yourself in situations that offer the Big Picture experience.

Ask: What Big Picture experiences can you create for yourself?

Make this a journey to remember …

**ORDER YOUR PRE-PRINTED
FEELINGS JOURNAL NOW!**
www.NormaT.xyz

www.ingramcontent.com/pod-product-compliance
Lightning Source LLC
Chambersburg PA
CBHW051936290426
44110CB00015B/2001